Wilhelm's School of Navigation

PREFACE

Compendium of Navigational Techniques is a handbook of navigational equations, written to be understandable to the professional mariner. Navigation is not presented as a mechanical process to be followed blindly. The emphasis is on the science that is used to effectively improve the *art* of navigation. It does not replace mature judgment and experience necessary to interpret information as it becomes available. Thus, modern equations are presented to help the mariner acquire perspective in meeting the various needs of seafarers as to their position.

Modern navigation techniques present the mariner with the opportunity to incorporate new timely mathematical equations and methods for self-preservation at sea. Early mariners used charted landmarks **(Piloting)** and **Dead reckoning** to predict their future positions. **Celestial navigation** was developed later to provide positions when charted landmarks were not available. **Electronic navigation** is the modern application of a different form of energy used to solve the position problem. Electronic equipment is used to extend the range of piloting.

Ocean navigation is the scientific process of directing the movement of a vessel from one point on the earth's surface to another as described by latitude and longitude. Modern scientific navigators need the tools required to lay a course and compute distance, a compass to steer by, and a means of determining vessel's position during passage.

This compendium of technical knowledge has been constructed and presented in order that a navigator process the tools to develop a voyage plan using dead reckoning, piloting techniques for position fixes, celestial equations for ocean passage, and tidal formula for a safe uneventful voyage. The primary result produced by this compendium is providing up-to-date, scientific navigation procedures applicable for small vessels. Some of these mathematical equations may seem complicated to the casual observer, however let me assure you that they are very convenient, and much quicker than graphic solutions and with more accuracy.

Bob Wilhelm
S/V Vaya Con Dios
Fort Pierce, Florida
13 April 2005

I0162485

i

Wilhelm's School Of Navigation

Acknowledgement for the effort and help provided by Barbara Del'Acqua, Dale Cawthorne, and Ed LeGere, I thank you all.

Wilhelm's School of Navigation

Wilhelm's School Of Navigation

Wilhelm's School Of Navigation

TEST SUBJECTS FOR MASTER/MATE
500/1600 TONS

Number of Questions: 10
Minimum Score: 90%

Subject	Mate 500/1600 (Module 215xx)	Master 500/1600 (Module 205xx)
Azimuth (Any Body)	√	√
Amplitude (Any Body)	√	√
Compass Error/Leeway	√	√
Speed By Rpm	√	√
Course In Current	√	
Compass Deviation		√
Electronic Navigation	√	√
Terrestrial Observations	√	√
Tide Problems	√	
Current Problems	√	
Course By Terrestrial Observation	√	√
Fuel Consumption		√
Zone Time Calculation		√

CELESTIAL NAVIGATION

Number of Questions: 15
Minimum Score: 80%

Subject	Mate 500/1600 (Module 215xx)	Master 500/1600 (Module 205xx)
Mid-latitude sailing	√	√
Mercator sailing	√	√
Great circle sailing	√	√
Parallel	√	√
Estimated Time of Arrival	√	√
Voyage Planning	√	√
Latitude by Polaris	√	√
Latitude by Meridian Transit (Sun)	√	√
Fix / Running Fix Sun	√	√
Fix / Running Fix Star	√	√
Time Meridian Transit (Sun)	√	√
Zone Time of Sun rise/set	√	√
Star Identification – Major	√	√
Star selection (Any Body)	√	√
Miscellaneous problems	√	√

Texas Instruments Calculator – TI-30Xa

Wilhelm's School Of Navigation

Most navigators use the Texas Instrument TI-30Xa because it's simplistic, easy to operate, and low in cost. Regional Examination Center, United States Coast Guard allows the TI-30Xa to be used when sitting for a maritime license. The TI-30Xa keys have dual function. The white keys are the primary keys accessed directly while the yellow secondary keys are accessed with the 2nd yellow key located in the upper left hand corner. This calculator contains three memories, which are written over, and never erased.

KEY	KEY	FUNCTION
ON/c		Turn on calculator
ON/c		Clear last entry and error
OFF		Turns calculator off
STO	1	Stores display in memory number 1
STO	2	Stores display in memory number 2
STO	3	Stores display in memory number 3
RCL	1	Recalls memory number 1 to display
RCL	2	Recalls memory number 2 to display
RCL	3	Recalls memory number 3 to display
2nd	DMS-DD	Degrees (.) minutes and seconds to decimal
2nd	DD-DMS	Turns decimal to degrees minutes and seconds
2nd	SIN	Trigonometric function Sine
2nd	COS	Trigonometric function Cosine
2nd	TAN	Trigonometric function Tangent
÷		Mathematical operation – divide
X		Mathematical operation – multiply
-		Mathematical operation – subtract
+		Mathematical operation – add
=		Mathematical operation – equal

The Texas Instrument TI-30Xa calculator is used to solve all navigation problems from Time to Celestial positions. Memorizing the navigation equations is easy when the navigator understand how this calculator operates. Before using **Degrees, Minutes, Seconds** (DMS) value in a calculator, it must be converted to decimal form, (DMS-DD). Any solution with **Hour, Minute, Second** in decimal form must be converted to time form, (DD-DMS).

Wilhelm's School of Navigation

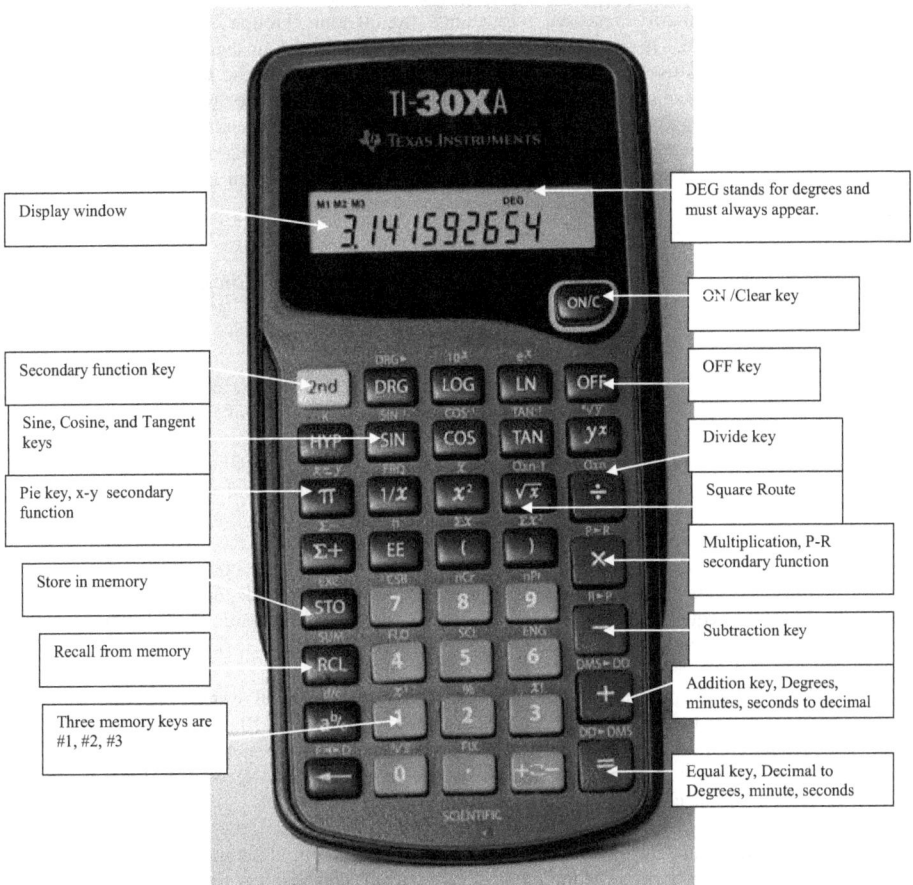

TI-**30X**A

Texas Instruments

M1 M2 M3   DEG

3.141592654

Display window

DEG stands for degrees and must always appear.

ON /Clear key

Secondary function key

OFF key

Sine, Cosine, and Tangent keys

Divide key

Pie key, x-y secondary function

Square Route

Store in memory

Multiplication, P-R secondary function

Recall from memory

Subtraction key

Three memory keys are #1, #2, #3

Addition key, Degrees, minutes, seconds to decimal

Equal key, Decimal to Degrees, minute, seconds

SCIENTIFIC

Wilhelm's School Of Navigation

TIME CONVERSION:

Time is customarily expressed in time units, from 0 hours through 24 hours, to the nearest minute. It is generally stated for navigation in a four-digit format. No punctuation is used. Thus 0000 or 2400 represents midnight the start of a day. Every 15° of Longitude, a standard meridian, measured from the prime meridian, Greenwich England, represents one hour. Each of these standard meridians determines zonetime, which is measured 7½° each side of a standard meridian. In this manner an entire zone has the same time, in contrast with apparent time, which uses celestial reference to measure actual solar passage.

TIME					ARC		
1 Day	=	24 hours	=	360°	=	1 Circle
60 minutes	=	One hour	=	15°		
		4 minutes	=	1°	=	60 minutes
60 seconds	=	1 minute	=	15 minutes		
		4 seconds	=	1 minute	=	60 seconds
		1 second	=	15 seconds	=	0.25 of a minute

Hours are whole numbers and can be added, subtracted, multiplied, or divided without conversion into decimal form. However, minutes and seconds are a different story since minutes and seconds represent a fraction of an hour. Some candidates for maritime licenses have difficulty understanding the need for time conversion. Time is computed in a base 60 system, which are 60 sub-units of a minute equals one main unit or one hour. The same for seconds, 60 sub-units or seconds is equal to one minute. The problem arises when computing speed, time, and distance equations.

Distance and speed are whole numbers, which use a base 10 system. All sub-units or fractions of speed or distance are units of 10 such as 10 dimes equal one dollar, a whole unit. In order to solve a time, speed and distance problem time must be converted to base 10; otherwise time is base 60 while speed and distance is base 10, the classic case of apples and oranges.

Since time must be converted to a base 10 system, the minutes and seconds are divided by 60 to arrive at the decimal equivalent. This result is time, speed and distance all being in a base 10 format. When a solution to an equation results in time it is in decimal format and must be converted to a base 60 format or time Minutes and seconds in decimal format, the numbers after the period multiplied by 60 results in minutes, and seconds. Hours are whole numbers and do not need conversion.

The Texas Instrument TI30Xa calculator will furnish the conversion of time into decimal, which is minutes and seconds of time divided by 60. This may be accomplished with the 2nd and DMS-DD keys. Enter the hour or hours followed by a period, with minutes and seconds, then press 2nd DMS-DD keys. The result

Wilhelm's School Of Navigation

will be time in decimal format. To convert an answer in decimal hours, minutes, and seconds of time in decimal format, press the 2nd DD-DMS keys.

CONVERTING MINUTES, SECONDS TO DECIMAL FORM:
Prior to any mathematical operation with time, time must be converted into decimal form. The Texas Instrument TI-30Xa (non-solar) handles this conversion very simply as illustrated below.

KEY STROKES FOR TIME CONVERSION

KEY	KEY	DISPLAY	COMMENT
	ON/c	0.	Turn calculator to the on mode
.	30	0.30	Enter period prior to 30 minutes
2nd	DMS-DD	0.5	Conversion of 30 minutes to a decimal
	OFF		Turns calculator to the off mode

As you can see from the above illustration the calculator divided the 30 minutes by 60 resulting in the decimal of 0.5 or 50%. The digits after the number 0.5 are understood as 0.50000.

One hour, 30 minutes, 30 seconds would be entered as follows:

KEY STROKES FOR TIME CONVERSION

KEY	KEY	DISPLAY	COMMENT
	ON/c	0.	Turn calculator to the on position
1.	3030	1.3030	Enter period after hour prior to 30m 30s
2nd	DMS-DD	1.50833333	Conversion to decimal form
	OFF		Turns calculator to the off mode

DECIMAL TIME TO HOURS MINUTES SECONDS:
The result of time obtained from a mathematical operation is in decimal form and of little use to the navigator. Therefore decimal time must be converted into the time format as shown.

KEY STROKES FOR TIME CONVERSION

KEY	KEY	DISPLAY	COMMENT
		0.5	Result of 3 miles divided by 6 knots
2nd	DD-DMS	0°30'00"	Conversion of 0.5 to 30 minutes
	OFF		Turns calculator to the off mode

LATITUDE AND LONGITUDE CONVERSION:
A map is conventionally used to illustrate the topography of the earth's land surface. Nautical charts are intended for marine navigation exhibiting water depth, aids to navigation, danger areas, and the outline of adjacent landmasses with important land features. Nautical charts are classified by how the projection

Wilhelm's School Of Navigation

of the earth's round surface is accomplished on a flat surface, and this results in different types of charts. The most common projection used for marine navigation is called **Mercator** with degrees of latitude and longitude intersecting at right angles. This is an important advantage because a course line on a Mercator projection is a **Rhumb** line showing the true course; however a straight line is not a **Great Circle** route (shortest distance between points on earth's surface). Other projections a mariner may use are **Lambert Conformal** or a **Polyconic** where a straight line drawn on this chart is a great circle route.

The length of a line drawn on a Mercator chart is normally measured in nautical mile, to the nearest 0.1 miles. Use the latitude scale found on either side of the chart for measuring distance or on the bar scale found at the chart bottom. One minute of latitude is equal to a mile, which is 2,025 yards or 6076 feet. Near the equator a ship traveling 180 miles by measurement on the chart would cover only 179 miles over the earth surface. The reason for this difference is Mercator projections do not allow for a great circle measurement.

The earth's surface is overlaid with a grid used to describe positions. The three primary divides are (1) the **equator**, (zero degree of latitude) which divides the North Hemisphere from the Southern Hemisphere, and is measured from the equator 0° to 90° north or 90° south, (2) **Prime meridian,** located at Greenwich, England (zero degree of longitude) divides the East and West hemispheres and is measured 180° east and 180°west to the **International Date Line.**

Degrees of latitude and longitude are further divided into minutes and seconds with latitude scale located on both sides of a chart while the longitude scale is located at top and bottom of the chart. Both the latitude and longitude scales on Coastal Charts show degrees, minutes and tenth of minutes. Tenth of minutes must be converted to seconds to arrive at an accurate mathematical solution when using the TI30Xa calculator. Degrees are whole numbers that may be divided, multiplied, added or subtracted without conversion into decimal format. Since minutes and seconds are a base 60 system (60 minute's equal one degree) they must be converted to decimal format.

To exemplify the previous mathematical problem let us consider finding the difference between 37°28.4N and 26°45.6N. The degrees may be subtracted normally; however we cannot take 45 minutes from 28minutes without increasing 28 minutes by a degree or 60 minutes. Also this same predicament exists with subtracting 6 tenths of minutes from 4 tenths. That is, 0.4 tenths of 60 seconds must be increased by 1 minute or 60 seconds, (0.4 X 6) + 60 = 84 seconds. Keeping in mind the need to increase minutes and seconds, this mathematical problem can be restated.

$$36°\ 87'\ 84"N$$
$$\underline{26°\ 45'\ 36"N}$$
$$10°\ 42'\ 48"$$

Wilhelm's School Of Navigation

As you may observe one degree or 60 minutes was transferred to the 28 minutes, totaling 88 minutes. The same procedure was use for seconds, one minute or 60 seconds was transferred to the original 24 seconds totaling 84 seconds. This result is 36°87'84N which has the same value as 37°28.4N. To solve mathematical equations the minutes, and seconds of latitude or longitude must be converted from minutes and seconds into decimal format. To obtain maximum mathematical accuracy it is necessary to convert tenths of minutes to seconds prior to entry in the calculator. The Texas Instrument TI-30Xa calculator will solve latitude and longitude conversions quickly. Following are the keystrokes used to solve for this conversion.

KEY STROKES FOR LATITUDE/LONGITUDE CONVERSION

KEY	KEY	DISPLAY	COMMENT
	ON/c	0.	Turn calculator on
	37.2824	37.2824	Enter latitude 37°28.4N - (0.4 X 60 = 24")
2nd	DMS-DD	37.47333333	Latitude expressed in decimal form
2nd	DD-DMS	37°28' 24"	Latitude expressed in degree, minutes, & seconds
	OFF		Calculator turned off

Remember maximum mathematical accuracy is acquired with conversion of tenths of minutes to seconds prior to entry in the calculator. Since one tenth is equal to 6 seconds, we multiply the number of tenths by 60 to achieve the result. Using the calculator to calculate the difference between 37°28.4N, and 26°45.6N the following keystrokes are essential.

KEY STROKES FOR LATITUDE/LONGITUDE CONVERSION

KEY	KEY	DISPLAY	COMMENT
	ON/c	0.	Turn calculator on
	37.2824	37.2824	Enter latitude 37°28.4N (tenths to seconds)
2nd	DMS-DD	37.47333333	Latitude expressed in decimal form
-	26.4536	26.4536	Enter latitude 26°45.6N
2nd	DMS-DD	26.76	Latitude expressed in decimal form
	=	10.71333333	Difference in decimal format
2nd	DD-DMS	10°42'48"	Difference expressed in degree, minute & seconds
	OFF		Calculator turned off

DISTANCE TO HORIZON:

Official definition of horizon: That great circle of the celestial sphere midway between the zenith, [point of celestial sphere vertically overhead] and nadir, [point on celestial sphere vertically below observer] or a line resembling or

Wilhelm's School Of Navigation

approximating such a circle. More simply stated, the visible horizon is the furthest the eye can see earth's surface in any direction from a geographical point. Distance to the visible horizon depends on height of the eye. The higher the eye above earth's surface the greater the angle and the horizon is further away. Likewise, the smaller the angle the visible horizon is closer. When the angle is zero there is no visible horizon.

There are four main types of horizons, (1) **visible horizon**, [line where earth and sky meet] (2) **celestial horizon**, [passes thru center of earth perpendicular to zenith/nadir line] (3) **artificial horizon**, [device used to level sextant] and the **sensible horizon** [passes thru eye of observer perpendicular to zenith/nadir line]. The horizon system of coordinates is based upon the celestial horizon (also known as rational horizon). This is a great circle of the celestial sphere half way between the zenith and nadir. The celestial sphere is an imaginary artificial globe surrounding the earth where all stars and planets are considered situated to simplify celestial navigation.

Through this imaginary celestial sphere surrounding the earth a plane cutting through the center of the earth intersects the celestial sphere midway between the zenith and nadir resulting in the celestial horizon. An eye at 90° north, for example, the geodetic North Pole, looking horizontally straight out does not see the horizon but the sky, this is known as the sensible horizon. When observing the visible horizon, (the sea-level surface edge of water), the visible horizon will be lower than the celestial horizon, which is midway between the zenith and nadir. The angle between the sensible horizon and visible horizon is known as **Dip**.

Celestial observation of the sun, moon, stars or planets is used for amplitudes. For your edification, amplitude is angular distance north or south of prime vertical; arc of horizon or angle between zenith and prime vertical. The amplitude is desirable because it measures the celestial body at a low altitude making the observation easy and more accurate. The following illustration displays horizons used.

Practical navigation requires the navigator to know the distance between his vessel and the horizon. The distance to the horizon provides an observer with a valuable relationship. Any vessel, target, or object between the observer and the horizon can be quickly estimated. Also the approximate geographic range an object will be come visible to an observer at sea level is an important navigation tool. It is necessary to add to the distance for the height of any object the distance corresponding to the height of the observer's eye above sea level.

Wilhelm's School Of Navigation

The mathematical equation, square root of height eye multiplied by the coefficient of 1.14, equals distance to horizon in miles as shown below.

$\sqrt{\text{Height of eye}}$ X   1.17 = Distance to horizon in miles

EXAMPLE: Determine the geographic visibility of an object, with a height above water of 5 feet, for an observer with a height of eye of 35 feet. The computation as follows:

$$\sqrt{5 \text{ X } 1.17} = 2.6M$$
$$\sqrt{35 \text{ X } 1.17} = \underline{7.2M}$$

Computed geographic visibility   9.8M

KEY STROKES FOR TI-30Xa CALCULATOR

KEY	KEY	DISPLAY	FUNCTION
	ON/c	0.	Turn calculator to the on mode
5	√X	2.236067978	Square route of 5
X	1.17	1.17	Multiply by coefficient
	=	2.549117494	Distance to horizon 2.5 miles
	OFF		Turn calculator to off mode

Wilhelm's School Of Navigation

NAVIGATOR'S DECK LOG

WAYPOINT Latitude Longitude	TK	L	TC	MC	SPEED	MILES	TTG	ETA	AT.

Wilhelm's School Of Navigation

CHARTS AND PUBLICATION:

Navigators need to know what charts and publications are available as they are an important source of navigational material. The U.S. Coast Pilot, published by NOAA, supplements navigational information shown on nautical charts. U.S. Coast Pilot is indispensable to safe navigation. Mariners must make the right decision at the right time.

First the navigator must have a source for charts and publications needed to carry out his voyage. There is no central government agency in charge of issuing all of the available charts and related publications. No, the Government Printing Office does not handle navigational material. The principal source for publications used by mariners is NOAA, Army Map Service, Coast Guard, Naval Observatory, and U.S. Engineer Office, Department of the Army. The best source for the navigator is retail authorized sales agent such as Blue Water Books, located in Fort Lauderdale, Florida for all their requirements. Webb site, www.Bluewater.com, or for Government publications, http=//bookstore.gpo.gov/index.html.

The National Oceanic and Atmospheric Administration maintains liaison with foreign hydrographic offices, which make topographic, oceanographic, and geomagnetic surveys in international waters and along foreign coasts. All research conducted in oceanographic and in navigational methods are compiled and published in print and through radio broadcasts for safe navigation. NOAA not only publishes nautical high seas charts, but also harbor charts, sailing directions, pilot charts, loran and radar charts, and plotting sheets. In addition, NOAA publishes the tide and current tables for the United States and its possessions and a number of special publications covering results of its research.

The United States Coast Guard is charged with the responsibility of inspection of merchant marine vessels, licensing merchant marine officers, installation and maintenance of aids to navigation (lighthouses, beacons, buoys, etc.). It publishes the **Light List** for United States waters, and international and inland rules of navigation together with **pilot rules**. This pamphlet provides the international rules, inland rules, western river rules, and Great Lake rules in parallel columns, followed by the pilot rules.

The United States Naval Observatory conducts research in various areas of astronomy, including measurement and dissemination of Universal Time. It publishes the **nautical and air almanacs**, as well as tables of sunrise, sunset, and twilight. The object of the nautical almanac is to provide, in a convenient form, the data required for the practice of astronomical navigation at sea. The main content of the almanac consists of data from which the *Greenwich Hour Angle* (GHA) and the *Declination* (Dec) of all the bodies used for navigation can be obtained for any instant of *Universal Time* (UT), or *Greenwich Mean Time* (GMT). The *Local Hour Angle* (LHA) can be calculated from the GHA by subtracting west longitude and adding east longitude.

Wilhelm's School Of Navigation

The U.S. Weather Bureau publishes pamphlets showing principal types of clouds, instructions for marine meteorological observers, glossary of weather terms, and other meteorological publications.

NOAA publishes **tide tables** annually. Webb site for tidal information, www.co-ops.hos.hoaa.gov. These tables tabulate the predicted times and heights of high and low waters for every day in the year at a number of reference stations. The time differences between the time of high and low water and the range of high and low water at various sub-stations is disclosed. Also the method for obtaining the height of the tide at any time, local mean time of sunrise and sunset for various latitudes are shown. Tide tables are available in separate volumes for (1) east coast of North and South America, including Greenland, (2) west coast of North and South America, including Hawaiian Islands, (3) Europe and west coast of Africa, including the Mediterranean Sea, and (4) central and western Pacific Ocean and Indian Ocean.

NOAA publishes annual tidal current tables. Current tables are tabulations of daily predictions of the times of slack water and the times and speed of maximum flood and ebb currents for a number of waterways. Other information is available on methods for obtaining speed of current at any time and the duration of slack water. Tidal current tables are available in separate volumes for (1) Atlantic coast of North America, and (2) Pacific coast of North America and Asia. For places not covered navigators must rely on other available source or sailing directions.

Pilot charts published each month for (1) Atlantic Ocean, and (2) the North Pacific Ocean. In addition, Pilot charts are published in atlas form for (1) North American Atlantic Ocean, (2) South Atlantic Ocean and Central American Waters, and (3) the South Pacific and Indian Ocean. The principal feature is monthly average for prevailing winds and currents. Percentage of gales, calms, and fog, together with lines of equal air and water temperature, and atmospheric pressure plus the drift limits of icebergs. These charts have lines of equal magnetic variation, location of ocean station vessels, and recommended routes of ship tracks.

Sailing Directions are books containing descriptions of coastlines, harbors, dangers, aids to navigation, winds, currents, and tides. Basic information for navigating narrow waterways approaches to harbors, port facilities, signal systems, pilot service and any other data that cannot be conveniently shown on the chart. Sailing directions covering the U.S. coast and or its possessions are called **Coast Pilot**, those covering foreign coasts are called sailing directions.

Light lists for the U.S. and or its possessions published semiannually depict all lighted and unlighted aids to navigation. The light List is corrected electronically each monthly. Updates to the Light List, **Local Notice to Mariners,** displays temporary changes and or corrections to the light list, and is no longer published weekly by U.S. Coast Guard in paper form. Web site,

Wilhelm's School Of Navigation

http=/chartmaker.ncd.noaa.gov/staff/charts.hjm. **Notice to Mariners** shows changes and or corrections to foreign navigation aids, and is published weekly in paper form.

Nautical Charts:

Nautical charts are graphic representation of the earth's sphere on a plane, that is, a flat surface. Maps are used for land travel, conversely charts are used for water navigation. Navigational charts illustrate shoreline, water depth, topographic features, and aids to navigation, danger areas, and other information of interest to navigators. A nautical chart presentation of the area of interest is one of the most essential and reliable aids available to the navigator.

Generally all nautical charts used for ordinary navigation are **Mercator projections** except for Great Lakes. These charts are constructed on various scales. Mariners should choose and use largest scale charts available of voyage area illustrating a small area with greatest detail. A nautical chart scale is expressed as a ratio, such as 1:80,000, which means for every inch on the chart it represents 80,000 inches on earth's surface. The larger the denominator the larger the area with less detail. For example, harbor charts are generally on a 1:50,000 scale or larger providing a small area with enormous detail. Small-scale charts covering large areas are used for planning and for offshore course plotting. Charts of large scale, covering smaller areas, should be used as vessel approaches pilot waters.

Nautical charts have two **datum** numbers. **Vertical datum** and a **horizontal datum**. The vertical datum or tidal datum is a level from which heights and water depths are measured. The most important reference to the mariner is the datum of soundings. There are two vertical water datum's, **mean low water**, which is the average depth of all low waters at given location, usually over 19 years. About half of low water depth will fall below the average. **Mean lower low water** is the average depth of the lower low water at a specific location. Actual water depth can be less than the mean lower low water datum. The second of the two datum's is a point called the horizontal datum, located in the center of the United States. This reference point provides for chart correlation, and allows for continuity of latitude and longitude between different charts. When setting up a Global Positioning receiver (GPS) the navigator must make sure that the chart datum (horizontal datum) is the same as the GPS datum.

The shoreline shown on nautical charts is the mean high-water line not the mean higher high-water line. Therefore, measurement of the **heights** of lighthouses, bridges, rocks, and other structures depicted on charts is from sea level (high-water). However, heights of islands, especially those some distance off the coast, are often taken from sources other than original hydrographic surveys, and may be reckoned from some other level, often mean sea level. Most of the time the plane of reference for topographic detail is not stated.

Wilhelm's School Of Navigation

The tremendous advantage of Mercator projections over other chart projections is plotting of a rhumb line (straight line) course. A true course line intersects all meridian at the same angle is a **rhumb line**. This enables the navigator to extract a true compass course directly from the chart. As opposed to a great circle route (shortest distance on earth's surface), which is a series of line segments intersecting meridians at different angles. Rhumb line sailing is most practicable for distances of less than 500 to 600 miles.

CHART NO. 1 contains all symbols, abbreviations, and terms used by [National Oceanic and Atmospheric Administration (NOAA)], and National Geo-spatial intelligence Agency on nautical charts. In January, 1975 the U.S. Government began producing nautical charts in meters. Since then, some charts have been issued with soundings and contours in meters. However, for the present, many charts are issued depicting soundings in feet, fathoms, or meters.

All points, lines, and, course changes must be labeled. H.H. Shufeldt and G.D. Dunlap standardize the labels commonly used in marine navigation in Hobbs Marine Navigation 1, and Piloting and Dead Reckoning. Only standard labels should be used. The principal rules for labeling points and vectors on DR plots are based on fix, course, and speed.

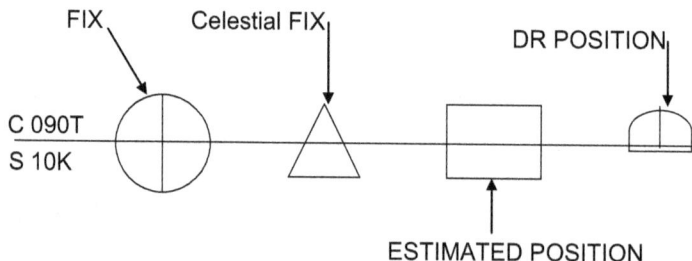

Plotting and labeling on a chart is important in order for the navigator to maintain a clear picture as to the vessel's progress over the earth's surface. True course is labeled above the line with vessel's speed below the course line. The time of a DR position or a fix is placed along side the mark. Lines of position (LOP) are labeled with time (24 hour method) above the line and the true bearing below the line.

When a chart is received, the date to which it has been hand corrected will be found stamped in the margin. Responsibility for maintaining corrections or changes lies with the navigator or master. An uncorrected chart can be extremely hazardous and a menace. The subsequent issues of Notice to Mariners to the stamped margin date contain all information needed to maintain correct charts. Urgent corrections are broadcast by Coast Guard radio. Permanent corrections should be made in ink so inadvertent erasure will not spoil the chart.

Wilhelm's School Of Navigation

HORIZONTAL DIRECTION MEASUREMENT:

On nautical charts horizontal measurement of direction is expressed as an angle from **geographic North** or the angle from **Magnetic North**. The referenced direction, generally true north, is the difference between the vessel's course and a meridian of longitude. In other words the vessel's true course line crosses all meridians at the same angle, measured in the number of degrees difference. A True Course is plotted in reference to the geographic north which is 90° north while a Magnetic Course is plotted with reference to the north magnetic core within the earth. Relative bearings are referenced to the vessels bow. It is the heading of the vessel bow, regardless of compass direction. For amplitudes, the reference direction is east or west, usually 090° or 270° true.

The compasses commonly used by mariners are either *gyroscopic* showing true course or *magnetic* showing magnetic course direction. A **magnetic compass** always points to magnetic north while the gyroscopic or **gyro compass** points to the geographic north. These compasses must have desirable characteristics to adequately serve its purpose as the vessel's steering compass. The most important characteristic is accuracy. No other quality, however important, can compensate for lack of accuracy. This does not mean that the steering compass needs to be without error, but any error must be known and or readily determined. The navigator must make provision for removing *deviation* (magnetic compass error) or reducing it to a minimum.

The compass designated as the **standard steering compass (Psc)** must be installed in an exposed position having an unobstructed view in most directions, permitting accurate determination of error. After the compass has been installed, proper adjustment and compensation should not be neglected. The modern gyrocompass has superseded the magnetic compass on most ships with a magnetic backup compass located where metal or electric circuits least affect it. In the American maritime it is wise to keep a record of errors and performance of the ship's gyrocompass on every watch.

The magnetic compass bowl is manufactured from a nonmagnetic material such cast bronze. Likewise, the compass card is also composed of a light, nonmagnetic material graduated in increments of degrees totaling 360. Unlike the gyro compass, which requires a great deal of maintenance and electric power to operate, the magnetic compass is essentially simplistic since it is independent of any power supply and can survive major damage to its ship without losing its utility. Small boat compasses often remain serviceable under the most rigorous conditions.

Despite the magnetic compass having great reliability it is subject to limitations. It responds to any magnetic field, and it is affected by any change in the local magnetic situation. Thus any magnetic material introduced near a compass will introduce unknown errors. These errors may be instituted by steel tools, steel cans, or by a change in position of a steel boom in the vicinity of a magnetic compass. Even such small amounts of magnetic material as a pocketknife, keys, or even nylon clothing will upset the magnetic field. Errors can occur when repairs or changes of equipment, especially electronic equipment is made or if the vessel is struck by lightning or if a short circuit occurs near the compass.

The directive force acting upon a magnetic compass is strongest at or near the magnetic equator, decreasing to zero at the magnetic poles. Therefore, at or near the magnetic poles a magnetic compass is useless.

It is most desirable to have a gyrocompass or magnetic compass for observing bearings or lines of position (LOP), however it may not be cost effective. Satisfactory results can be obtained by means of an inexpensive device known as a **pelorus** (dumb compass). In appearance the pelorus resembles a magnetic compass card or a gyrocompass repeater. A pelorus comes with a fixed compass card, and sighting vanes or sighting telescope attached. The compass card does not rotate or posses any directional properties. The card's North, 360°/000°, is in line with the vessel's **lubber's** line or keel making all observed angles, **relative.** By marking the vessel's course at the same time a bearing is observed by the pelorus; a relative bearing may be converted to a true bearing and plotted as an line of position (LOP).

A pelorus is useful in determining the moment at which an aid to navigation is broad on the beam. It is also useful in measuring pairs of relative bearings for use in determining distance off at second bearing and distance abeam, or obtaining a fix by observing two or more bearings and plotting two or more lines of position (LOP). Of course, if the true heading is set on the pelorus compass card to the lubber's line, true bearings are then observed directly without correction.

The easy way is to have the helmsman indicate when the vessel is on course. This is accomplished by calling out "mark, mark" as long as vessel is on course. The observer, who is watching a distant object across the pelorus, selects an instant when the vessel is steady on course. An alternative method is to have observer call "mark" when relative is steady, and helmsman notes ships heading. Each navigator must determine for himself or herself which technique produces the most reliable result.

Another device used for obtaining bearings of distant objects is the hand-held-compass. A hand-held-compass is a small magnetic compass that is easily portable, and small enough to fit the hand with a sighting notch or line. A navigator is able to stand in a convenient location aboard the vessel observing magnetic bearing of distant objects. The bearing observed is magnetic and must be converted to a true bearing prior to plotting. Therefore magnetic variation, if east must be added, and if west, subtracted to or from the observed magnetic bearing. Deviation, (*compass error*), is ignored since it will vary a great deal from location to location as to where the navigator stands. Of course when

Wilhelm's School Of Navigation

deviation is ignored, the resulting bearing is not as accurate, and this fact should be taken into consideration by the navigator.

Compass Errors:

The theory behind magnetism is the fact that iron can be provided with the ability to attract other iron material. This has been known for thousands of years. However the explanation of this phenomenon only occurred when knowledge of atomic structure was discovered. The magnetic field created around an electrical wire carrying electrical current and the magnetism of a permanent magnet is the result of the same phenomenon. Iron contains microscopically small regions, called **domains**. Within the domain an electrical field is created by electrons spinning around their atomic nuclei resulting in magnetized iron. The direction of domains in unmagnetized iron is arranged in a random manner as they relate to each other. In a strong magnetic field all of the domains rotate as much as 180° so as to become parallel to the "crystal axis" which is nearly parallel to the field's direction. When the strength of the magnetic field is increased sufficiently it induces the domains to rotate into parallelism with field, and the iron is magnetically saturated.

Magnetism, which exists only when influenced by an external magnetic field, is known as **induced magnetism**. When the external magnetic field is removed some magnetism remains, and is called **residual magnetism**. Iron that has been exposed to a very strong magnetic field so that all domains are aligning will retain for long periods its magnetism without appreciable reduction in strength. **Permanent magnetism** exists when iron contains their domain alignment for a very long period, and is used in the manufacture of marine compasses.

The area of an iron magnet where magnetic lines of force leave is called the **South Pole**, and the area where these lines of force enter the iron magnet is known as the **North Pole**.

The earth has a magnetic field; with its magnetic poles being located a distance from the geographical poles. When a permanent magnetize iron bar is suspended so it can turn feely, both horizontally and vertically, as in a compass, it aligns itself with the earth's magnetic field. When two magnets are mated end to end, unlike poles attract each other and like poles repel.

Another compass more modern than a magnetic compass is the gyrocompass. Naturally a man made manufactured compass is subject to error. This error called **gyro error (GE)** is expressed in degrees east or west to indicate the direction in which bearing is off set from true north. If the gyro error is east, the readings are too low; and if it is west, they are too high. Thus, if the gyro error (GE) is west it is subtracted from all compass readings, and added to all true directions to determine the equivalent gyro direction.

Wilhelm's School Of Navigation

There are two different types of magnetic compass errors, **variation** and **deviation**. Variation is the difference between the geographic North Pole, which is 90° north and the magnetic north pole. Remember a magnetic compass points toward the north magnetic field of the earth. A rhumb line drawn on a Mercator projection may be labeled true or magnetic. If it is true the rhumb line intersects all meridians at the same angle as related to geographic north. A rhumb line related to geographic north drawn on a chart is either a true course line **(TC)** or a line of position **(LOP)** or bearing. The true course (TC) measures the direction from a departure latitude/longitude to the destination latitude/longitude as it relates to geographic north. A line of position (LOP) on the other hand is a bearing or direction as it related to geographic north on which the observer observes some navigational mark or hazard.

Deviation is simply the error of a particular magnetic compass at a specific location at a specific time on a specific heading. Deviation is different on each heading while variation is the same on all headings. The Deviation error is the result of magnetic material or electronic fields in the area of a magnetic compass affecting its performance. As these materials change, and with additional electronic fields created over time so does the Deviation error.

On a chart all course lines and lines of position should be drawn in relation to geographic north as a true course (TC) or true bearings (LOP). Once the true course has been established mathematically or by direct measurement it must be uncorrected for the helmsman to steer. The un-correcting process is accomplished by using a work form: *T V makes dull children add wisdom.* "T" stands true, "V" stands for variation, "M" stands for magnetic compass, "D" stands for deviation, "C" stands for compass course, and "W" stands for add west variation and deviation, which means subtracting east variation and deviation. Likewise the compass course can be corrected with the work form: *can dead men vote twice at elections* "C" stands for compass course, "D" stands for deviation, "M" stands for magnetic compass, "V" stands for variation, "T" stands for true course, and at elections "E" stands for add east.

To obtain the Steering-Compass-Course (CC) another error occurs that affects the compass course, called leeway (L). Leeway is the result of set, and drift, a force exerting pressure, which causes the vessel to go off its course line. The complete work form to un-correct a true course appears as:

TC	L	TCOG	V	MCOG	D	CC

The variation error may be found within the magenta colored compass rose printed on charts. The outer ring provides 360 degrees of true bearings while the inner ring, on coastal charts, supplies 360 degrees of magnetic bearings. Within the magenta compass rose, inside the inner circle, the variation is given in degrees and minutes, and applicable year. On the next line, the minutes of annual increase

Wilhelm's School Of Navigation

or decrease in the variation error is disclosed. In addition to the degrees and minutes of variation shown is followed by the letter W or E, as appropriate. West variation is added to a true course while East is subtracted to arrive at magnetic course. Charts will contain several compass roses printed in various areas. The navigator must use the closes compass rose to his area which will contain the appropriate variation.

To compute the current year variation subtract year of variation indicated from current year. This difference is multiplied by the minutes of increase or decrease, which is used to correct the indicated variation to current year rounding minutes to nearest degree where appropriate.

True compass plus or minus leeway errors create concern for navigators. The ship's steering compass is not equivalent to direction taken from a chart. Direction taken from a chart is relative to the northerly direction along a geographic meridian. Ship's *course (track)* should be plotted and logged as true and adjusted for *variation, deviations,* and external force of wind or sea to obtain the *compass course to steer* Each compass is equipped with a *lubber line* that is horizontally mounted and oriented with ship's *keel* so that the vessel is headed in the direction, course over ground (COG), thereby making good its intended track.

UN-CORRECTING COMPASS COURSE:
Un-correcting a **true course (TC)** is the method used to find a **compass course (CC)**. There are two errors, Variation and deviation, that must be applied to the true course (TC) to calculate the compass course (CC). **Variation** is the angular difference between true north, and the direction of magnetic north at a given point on earth's surface. Variation is "east" when the observer is west of zero variation, and variation is "west" when the observer is east of zero variation. Or stated another way, when your compass points west toward magnetic north, variation is west, and when your compass points east toward magnetic north, variation is east. **Deviation** is the error in a magnetic compass caused by local magnetic influences. Simply stated, deviation is the error of a specific compass on a specific heading. Deviation is labeled "east" or "west" as the compass points east or west of magnetic north.

Variation is the same on all 360° compass headings, it does not change with vessels heading. However deviation may be different on each of the 360° compass headings. Deviation depends on the vessel's heading because there are two magnetic forces affecting and distorting the earth's magnetic field. The earth's magnetic force is imprecise due to local magnetic forces on board exerting energy effecting induced magnetism.

The work form "*TV makes dull children, add wisdom*" means T = true course, V = variation, M = magnetic course, D = deviation, and C = compass course. Add wisdom means add west variation and subtract east variation. The deviation error

Wilhelm's School Of Navigation

is handled exactly like variation, add west and subtract east deviation when un-correcting the true course (TC) to compass course (CC).

Example: The watch officer aboard the bulk carrier, Texas Arrow, on a true course (TC) of 135°T needs to calculate the vessel's compass course (CC) when variation is 15° west, and deviation is 7° east. Following is the work form necessary to solve for compass course.

T	TC	135°T	True Course
V	V	015W	Variation add west
Makes	MC	150°MC	Magnetic Compass
Dull	D	007E	Deviation subtract east
Children	CC	143°CC	Compass Course

Add wisdom means add west variation/deviation, subtract east variation/deviation when un-correcting compass

CORRECTING COMPASS COURSE:

Correction of a compass course (CC) is the opposite of un-correcting, that is starting with the compass course (CC) making adjustments for deviation (D) and variation (V) resulting in the true course (TC). To accomplish a compass correction a navigator must interpolate, produce an accurate value of deviation. Every ship must have on board a table showing deviation every 15°. A dilemma develops when the navigator must choose; interpolate the amount of deviation between 5° of deviation and 15° of compass bearings.

This is explained much better with an extraction from a deviation table:

DEVIATION TABLE

Magnetic Compass	Deviation
045°	5° W
060°	8°W

As you may see a problem develops when we need the deviation value for 050° since a compass heading does not appear. A navigator must then interpolate this value from the *Deviation Table*. The interval between tabular entries is 15 degrees, and the difference between deviation values is 3 degrees. Since 050° is 5/15ths of the spread between 045° and 060°, we can multiply the deviation difference 3° by $5/15^{th}$, which is a third, or 1°. Therefore, *deviation* is (5° + 1°) or 6° total which is added to 050°, or 056°CC.

Many times a fraction results when interpolating, for example: what is the deviation when the compass heading is 053°? Now the fraction is 8/15ths multiplied by 3°, or 1.6. Since only whole degrees can be steered by compass, the 1.6 is rounded to 2°, then added (5°+2°=7° and subtracted from 053° making the

Wilhelm's School Of Navigation

magnetic compass (MC) value 046°. Remember we add west variation and deviation when un-correcting and subtract when correcting.

The work form *Can Dead Men Vote Twice at elections* is and easy way to remember *Can* = compass course (CC), *Dead* = deviation (D), *Men* = magnetic compass (MC), *Vote* = variation (V), and *Twice* = true course (TC). At election tell us to add east when correcting the compass.

Example: The watch officer aboard the bulk carrier, Texas Arrow, on a compass course (CC) of 143°C needs to calculate the vessel's true course (TC) when variation is 15° west, and deviation is 7° east. Following is the work form necessary to solve for compass course. Note east is added and west is subtracted when calculating from CC to TC.

Twice	TC	135	True Course
Vote	V	015W	Variation add west
Men	MC	150	Magnetic Compass
Dead	D	007E	Deviation subtract east
Can	CC	143	Compass Course

One of two magnetic compass errors, *variation* is the angular difference between true north and magnetic north. This difference caused by terrestrial magnetism, known as *variation* (V) is the same on all points of the compass. Variation error is published on navigational charts inside the magnetic compass rose. Variation is revealed and valid only on the date of chart publication. It is shown in degrees, labeled east or west, along with annual minutes of increase or decrease. It is named east or west to indicate if variation is to be added or subtracted to or from true north. *Uncorrecting* for the variation from true north, algebraic signs " (-) or (+) " are specified respectively for east and west.

Magnetic Compass (MC) is the result obtained from subtracting or adding variation to or from true north, (uncorrecting). A navigator must first compute the amount of variation to be applied. To obtain this correction multiply the difference in years by the minutes shown in the compass rose. This results in the amount of variation to be added to or subtracted from true *course*

Example: The cruse ship Ecstasy is underway from Charleston to Liverpool, steering a true course of 037°, on July 4, 1990. The annotations inside the compass rose, on a chart dated 1985, shows 6° of west variation with 5' increase at this latitude. What Is the Magnetic Course to steer?

Year	Degree	Increase
1990	06° 00'	
1985	00° 25'	5' X 5 years
0005	06° 00'	

Variation is 06° 00' west because 25' is less than 30', half a degree.

Wilhelm's School Of Navigation

Ship's Course or track	(TC)	037°
Variation	(V)	006° W
Magnetic Course	(MC)	043°

Deviation (Dev) is the angular difference between magnetic north (MC) and compass north (CC). It is expressed in degrees and labeled east or west to indicate if this error is to be subtracted (east) or added (west). The deviation error is different on each point of the compass. Iron or electrical fields that influence the magnetic field cause this difference (deviation) of a particular magnetic compass course. Result is a course that indicates something other than the magnetic course (MC).

> *Example:* The cruse ship Ecstasy is underway from Charleston to Liverpool, steering a course of 037°, on July 4, 1990. The annotations inside the compass rose, on a chart dated 1985, shows 6° of west variation with 5' increase at this latitude. Deviation on this heading is 3° E . What Is the Compass Course to steer?

SOLUTION FOR UNCORRECTING COMPASS

TC	V	MC	D	CC
037°	6° W	043°	3° E	040°

Leeway is the result of an external force, ensuing from current and or wind, exerting a leeward motion on the vessel. Leeway may be expressed as angular difference between course steered and track. The external force varies with speed and relative direction of wind, type of vessel, amount of freeboard, trim, and speed of vessel, sea state, and water depth. Most convenient method of applying leeway is adding or subtracting its effect to compass course (CC). Leeway is the result of computing the effects of set and drift and when applied to the compass course (CC) provides the per steering course (psc). The direction, in which the water is moving, direction of push, is called *set,* and the speed of the set (current) is called *drift.*

When the relative motion of the set pushes on the starboard side of a vessel the algebraic sign (+) is assigned. Similarly when the relative effect of the set exerts its force on the port side the algebraic sign (-) is assigned. Therefore we need to determine on which side the dominant force exerts its influence.

> *Example:* The cruse ship Ecstasy is underway from Charleston to Liverpool, steering a track of 037°, on July 4, 1990. The annotations inside the compass rose, on a chart dated 1985, shows 6° of west variation with 5' increase at this latitude. Deviation on this heading is 3° E . Leeway was computed to be 7° with wind on port side of vessel. What Is the Compass Course to steer?

SOLUTION FOR UNCORRECTING COMPASS

Tr	L	COG	V	MC	D	CC
037°	-7°	030°	6° W	036°	3°E	033°

Wilhelm's School Of Navigation

Dead Reckoning:

Dead reckoning (DR) navigation is determining a vessels position by advancing a known position along the course line a calculated distance. Distance is computed using the vessel's speed through the water as opposed to speed over the bottom. The direction or course advanced from a known position should always be the true course steered since it produces less confusion when all directions are common. Thus, geographically, a dead reckoning position is an approximate vessel position corrected when possible with a fix.

The navigator can obtain a better idea as to the vessel's position when those elements that introduce geographical error into the dead reckoning position are taken into consideration. This type of navigation is known as an **estimated position (EP)**. EP navigation is applies an estimated correction to the dead reckoning position or by estimating the course and speed made good over the bottom, known as **course over ground (COG)**. It is a good practice to keep estimated reckoning distinct from dead reckoning thereby eliminating confusion or to provide a basis for evaluating the accuracy of the estimates.

Because dead reckoning is the bases for all navigation, its importance cannot be overstated. Watch Officers must maintain a careful log of all courses and speeds, times of all changes, and compass errors. Many navigators keep their recordings of dead reckoned positions by plotting directly on the chart by drawing lines or vectors to represent direction and distance of travel. From time to time or parallel with dead reckoning an estimated position will be calculated. This method is simple and direct and was widely practiced when charts were inexpensive. On large ships with a chart table, charts are reusable by plotting directly on tracing paper that overlay the chart. However, on smaller vessels, 50 tons or less, where navigation space is unavailable or at a premium, positions are computed mathematically and recorded in a Quartermaster or Watch Officer's log.

The necessity of accurate dead reckoning navigation becomes apparent when the time of sunrise and sunset, and which celestial bodies are available for observation is required. Also, the prediction of available electronic aids to navigation, the suitability and interpretation of soundings for position determination, predicting times of landfall, sighting lights, **estimate of arrival time (ETA)**, and the evaluation of fixed positions entail detailed dead reckoning navigation. Large errors are often apparent as inconsistencies in an otherwise regular plot. Keeping dead reckoning mathematically is the most precise.

The true course may be read directly from a Mercator chart, and the distance may be measured along the course line. The resulting course line is a rhumb line as opposed to a great circle, which is more desirable. Additionally, there usually is about a tenth difference between distance measured and distance calculated mathematically. The mathematical formula to advance a Dead Reckoning Position and solution for time, speed, distance is presented in the next paragraphs.

TIME, SPEED, DISTANCE FORMULA:

"D" is distance in miles, "T" is time in minutes, and "S" is speed in knots. The three basic equation for calculating *Time, Speed, Distance,* where time must be expressed in minutes are as follows:

$$D = \frac{S \times T}{60} \qquad S = \frac{60 \times D}{T} \qquad T = \frac{60 \times D}{S}$$

EXAMPLE:

To find the **time to go (TTG)** where distance equals 15 miles and speed equals 10 knots:

$$T = \frac{60D}{S} = \frac{60 \times 15 \text{ miles}}{10 \text{ knots}} = 90 \text{ minutes or 1 hour 30 minutes}$$

The following form is a simple way to remember when to divide or multiply. Place your finger over what you need answered, that is, the "D", "S", or "T", and then completes the math. Minutes of time must be converted to decimal form (minutes ÷ 60) prior to multiplication or division and the answer converted to time format (minutes X 60) when distance is divided by speed.

$$\frac{D}{S \times T}$$

SOLUTION USING TI-30Xa Calculator

KEY	KET	DISPLAY	FUNCTION
Find distance traveled in 1h 30m at a speed of 12 knots.			
1.30	2nd DMS-DD	1.5	Decimal hours
X	12	12	Multiply by speed
=		18	Equals distance 18M
Find time to go a distance of 18 miles at 12 knots.			
18	÷	18	Distance
12	=	1.5	Decimal hours
2nd	DD-DMS	1°30'00"00	Time 0130 hours
Finding speed when distance traveled is 18 Miles in 01h 30m.			
18	÷	18	Distance
1.30	2nd DMS-DD	1.5	Decimal time
=		12	Speed 12 knots

Wilhelm's School Of Navigation

ADVANCE DEAD RECKONING POSITION:

EXAMPLE: *A ship's speed is 19 knots for 3 hours, 14 minutes on a course of 258° from a DR position of 26°36.0S, 077°13.0E. What is the vessels position after traveling 61.4 miles?*

KEY	DISPLAY	FUNCTION	COMPUTATION
61.4	61.4	Enter distance	26°36.0S
2nd x-y	0.	Polar Rectangular	+ 12.7
258	258	Enter course	26° 48.7S Latitude
2nd P-R	-12.76577782	Difference of Lat.	26°36.0S
2nd x-y	60.05826269	Polar Rectangular	53° 24.7S ÷ 2
÷	60.05826269	Divide	26° 42.3S Mid-Lat. 27°
27°	27	Mid-Lat	
COS	0.89553786	Cosin	077°13.0E
=	-67.404964	Or 001°07.4W	001°07.4
			076°05.6E Longitude

NOTE #   North or south latitude, with increasing latitude (+ADD)
North or south latitude, with decreasing latitude (-SUBTRACT)
West or east longitude, with increasing longitude (+ADD)
West or east longitude, with decreasing longitude (-SUBTRACT)

CONSTRUCTION OF DEVIATION TABLE:

The precise technique for constructing a table of differences between a magnetic course and a compass course (Deviation) is to swing ship about a compass bearing every 15°. This may be accomplished by running different 15° headings across a range or by running the ship in a small circle recording the difference between sun's azimuth angle and compass bearing. Sun's azimuth angle or a range bearing must be observed through a sun compass or pelorus; a dumb compass, or compass card without a directive element mounted to provide bearings.

Example: *On January 5, 1981, when the ship was in DR latitude 21°42.0'S, Longitude 039°15.0'W, the **Amplitude** (Deviation) was observed with the sun's center on the Celestial Horizon, when the sun bore 270° PSC, variation for the locality was 19° west, chronometer read 09h 55m 40s, GMT, and was fast 00h 30m 30s. Determine the ship's deviation on this heading.*

Chronometer	09h 55m 40s	ZT.	1800	Dec.	22°32.7S (-0.3)
Chron. Error	-00h 30m 30s	ZD.	0300W	Corr.	-000°00.1
CCT	09h 25m 10s	GT	2100	Dec.	022°32.6S
	12h 00m 00s				
GMT	21h 25m 10s				

Wilhelm's School Of Navigation

CALCULATOR TI-30Xa

KEY	KEY	DISPLAY	FUNCTION
21.42	2nd DMS-DD	21.7	Latitude South
+∞-		-21.7	South set minus
STO	1	-21.7	Store memory 1
22.3236	2nd DMS-DD	22.54333333	Declination
+∞-		-22.54333333	South set minus
STO	2	-22.54333333	Store memory 2
90		90	"t" Angle
STO	3	90.	Store memory 3
RCL	2	-22.54333333	Recall memory 2
SIN	-	-0.383382062	Sin / subtract
RCL	3	90.	Recall memory 3
COS	X	0.	Cosin / multiply
RCL	1	21.7	Recall memory 1
SIN	=	-0.383382062	Sin / equal
÷		-0.383382062	Divide
RCL	3	90.	Recall memory 3
SIN	÷	-0.383382062	Sin / divide
RCL	1	-21.7	Recall memory 1
COS	=	-0.412623638	Cosin / equal
2nd	COS	114.3697545	Invert Cosin
-	360.	245.6302455	West subtract

TC	V	MC	D	CC
246	19W	265	5W	270

Speed is a dimension that can either be measured directly using logarithmic speed scale or calculated with knowledge of time and distance. A device such as a Chip Log or speedometer measures speed through the water. Speed over bottom is computed to the nearest tenth of a knot using (D) distance, and (T) time. A problem develops in time, speed, and distance calculations because time is base sixty mathematical system while distance and speed are a base tens system that is it takes 60 minutes to equal a whole hour, and 10 tenths to equal one mile.

SOLUTION USING TI-30Xa Calculator

KEY	KET	DISPLAY	FUNCTION
\multicolumn{4}{Find distance traveled in 1h 30m at a speed of 12 knots.}
1.30	2nd DMS-DD	1.5	Decimal hours
X	12	12	Multiply by speed
=		18	Equals distance 18M
\multicolumn{4}{Find time to go a distance of 18 miles at 12 knots.}
18	÷	18	Distance
12	=	1.5	Decimal hours
2nd	DD-DMS	1°30'00"00	Time 0130 hours

Wilhelm's School Of Navigation

Finding speed when distance traveled is 18 Miles in 01h 30m.			
18	÷	18	Distance
1.30	2nd DMS-DD	1.5	Decimal time
=		12	Speed 12 knots

NOAA charts with scale of 1:40,000 and larger have a Logarithmic speed scale.

1. To determine **speed (S)** set divider point on distance and the other point on time in minutes without changing divider span. Move divider so right point is on "60"; left point read speed.
2. To **resolve time to go (TTG)** a given distance for situations not exceeding one hour set one point on distance and other point on speed. Without changing divider span move divider, and place right point on "60"; left point read time in minutes.
3. Distance can be acquired from the logarithmic scale by setting the right point of dividers on "60" and the left point on speed without changing divider span. Move divider to time in minutes; left point indicates distance in miles.

Solutions for Time, Speed, Distance Problems:

$$D = \text{distance in miles}$$
$$S = \text{speed in knots}$$
$$T = \text{time in minutes}$$

$$D = \text{Speed} \times (\text{Time} \div 60) \qquad S = \frac{D}{(\text{Time} \div 60)} \qquad \text{Time } (T \times 60) = \frac{D}{\text{Speed}}.$$

Speed by *RPM* is the product of a set of speed trials that are run over a measured course, generally one mile for convenience. Most power vessels do not have marine speedometers, therefore engine *RPM* is used to determine speed. Engine tachometer provides revolutions per minute (RPM). A *speed curve* is prepared as a plot on graph paper of vessels speed for various engine RPM as shown by the tachometer. Located on some harbor charts a measured mile marked with buoys are made available for speed trials, however, when a marked measured mile is not available a GPS receiver will substitute. A measured course generally runs with and contrary to the current so that the effect of water speed may be averaged.

A speed curve (*RPM Table*) is computed by making repeated runs over a known distance using different throttle at even rpm settings. Generally each run is timed precisely and made twice, against and with the current. The distance run should be a convenient number for calculation, one to a half-mile. Anything less than a half-mile may produce timing errors that can grossly effect the speed calculation. It is important that each speed computation is run twice in each direction in order to average the time and eliminate the current effect.

Wilhelm's School Of Navigation

As each 1,000 RPM two way run is accomplished, measure the time for a carefully run direct course. When using a Texas Instrument calculator, TI-30Xa, the distance run is divided by the decimal equivalent of the sum of the two measured times. Each run is a separate calculation, added and averaged. Or the following time, speed, distance equation is solved algebraic. Where D represents distance run multiplied by 60, divided by minutes run equal speed.

$$\text{Speed} = \frac{60\text{Distance}}{\text{Time in minutes}}.$$

> Example: To clarify this equation, a practical problem will serve to make the solution memorable. A measure mile was run in both direction and the recorded time was 12 minutes and 18 minutes respectively for both runs. Therefore we multiply 60 by 1 and divide by 18, and then again 60 by 12, the result is averaged at 4 knots. Only nautical miles, (6076 feet), are used for maritime measurement of distance.

Applying the problem to a solution using the Texas Instrument calculator TI-30Xa the student needs to remember the equation and the following key strokes:

D = Distance
S = Speed
T = Time

$$\frac{D}{S \times T}$$

With a finger cover the desired answer. In our previous example, speed is the desired answer so with the "S" covered this leaves D divided by T visible. Time is a base 60 numerate and cannot be multiplied or divided until it is divided by 60 resulting in a decimal which is a base 10 numerate. To accomplish this computation the following keystrokes provides the solution.

Item	White Keys	Green / Brown Keys
Enter 18 minutes	.18	2nd (DMS-DD) +
Enter 12 minutes	.12	2nd (DMS-DD) =
Divide sum	.05	÷
Divide by 2 for average	2	=
Store minutes average	0.25	(STO) 1
Enter distance one mile	1	÷
Recall memory 1		(RCL) 1 =
Solution in knots	4	

NOAA charts with scale of 1:40,000, and larger have a logarithmic speed scale printed at bottom of chart. To use the scale, set one point of dividers on miles traveled and other divider point on time, in minutes. Without change to divider spread, set right end of divider point on 60 and read left divider point, the vessel's speed.

Wilhelm's School Of Navigation

A speed by RPM table is manufactured from a graph of the speed curve. On the left hand side of graph paper horizontally list the lowest to highest engine revolution. Left to right, across the bottom, list the time of run. Now, place a mark on the graph at the intersection of engine revolution and time. After entering all time runs, connect the marks using a French curve. A completed curve allows the navigator to prepare a table of vessel's speed at any interval of engine revolution.

Computing Speed/Engine Revolution Table:

Many sailing vessels have a marine speedometer aboard for determining **speed through the water (S).** Most power driven vessels do not have speedometers but compute their speed using specific engine settings. Engine speed is measured by the vessel's tachometer in **revolutions per minute (RPM).**

Revolutions per minute (RPM) can vary a great deal between a cargo loaded vessel and one that is empty. Also, the amount of fuel and water aboard affects weight. How these various loads are positioned aboard affects a vessel's performance. Therefore displacement and trim are of utmost importance. Condition of the ship's propeller and underwater hull, fouled with barnacles and or moss and slime will increase drag, slowing speed. These factors are necessary considerations when developing the RPM table.

Generally the vessel's speed will be computed for each 1000 increases in engine revolutions from approximately 500 RPM to maximum engine RPM. This speed run should be approximately one mile because watch errors have increased influence on the computation as the distance becomes shorter. Never have a run of less than half mile. You may use a measured mile established by the Coast Guard for such purposes or set up convenient GPS waypoints one mile apart for your speed run.

The speed trial must be run in one direction, timed, and computed then run 180° and computed. Thereby, allowing for the current effect. By running the same distance twice, 180° in each direction the results can be averaged. The averaged effect will be considered the tabulated speed at that RPM with a specific load. Following is the equation for solving for speed over a one-mile course with various times:

$$\text{Speed} = \frac{3600 \times \text{Distance}}{\text{Time (in seconds)}}$$

RPM	East – To - West		West – To - East		Average Speed
	Time	Speed	Time	Speed	
1000	6m – 45s	8.9	10m –52s	5.5	7.2
1500	5m – 35s	10.7	8m – 41s	6.9	8.8
1600	5m – 08s	11.7	6m – 53s	8.7	10.2

1700	4m – 53s	12.3	5m - 04s	11.8	12
1800	4m – 01s	14.9	4m – 45s	12.6	13.8
1900	3m – 53s	15.4	4m – 26s	13.5	14.4
2000	2m – 48s	21.4	3m – 56s	15.2	18.3
2200	2m – 21s	25.5	3m – 31s	17.1	21.3

A speed curve may be developed from the average speed, providing data at every engine setting. Construction of the *Engine Revolution Table* relates only to a certain condition of the vessel's bottom circumstance, fuel and water together with cargo aboard.

Computation of Vessel's ETA:

Estimating the time of arrival at a port within the vessel's time zone and on the same day does not present a problem. However, an obstacle occurs when the **estimated time of arrival (ETA)** exceeds a 24 hour period; now, you must account for days of travel as well as the hours and minutes. A ship traveling east or west an appreciable distance will cross one or more time zones. The secret is to keep our calculation simple. Convert local time to Greenwich Time, adding the time in route, and then converting Greenwich Time to zone-time at the destination.

Sound simple enough, but how is the zone-time calculated without looking on a time chart? Since every 15° east or west of Greenwich England equals one hour, we divide longitude by fifteen degrees. An example, departure longitude 075°58.0'W is divided by 15 degrees which results in time difference 05h 03' 52" or +5 **Zone Description (ZD)**.

Now that we know the time of departure in Greenwich Mean Time (GMT), the calculation is made by dividing distance by speed resulting in time in route. By adding the time in route to departure time the estimated time of arrival is computed. Change GMT to **Zone Time (ZT)** and our problem is solved.

Following is an outline of the step method:
1. Departure Longitude ÷ 15°   = Zone Description (ZD)
2. Departure time +/- ZD   = Greenwich Mean Time (GMT)
3. Distance ÷ Speed   = TTG in hours, and minutes
4. Hours ÷ 24   = Number of Days in route
5. Convert decimal hours to Readable Time
6. Add Days, Hours and Minutes to Departure Time
7. Convert GMT to zone time (ZT)

EXAMPLE:
The U.S. submarine Sea Poacher (SS406) leaves Cape Henry Buoy, Lat. 36°55.0'N, 075°58.0'W on 8 August 1999, at 0800, for the Mediterranean Sea. Course is set for a waypoint Lat. 30°N, Lo 20W, distance 2,792.4 nautical miles, course 081°T, speed 12k. What is the ETA at the waypoint?

Wilhelm's School Of Navigation

ITEM	DAY	TIME
ZT	8/8/99	0800
ZD EDT +4		0400
GMT		1200
TTG (2,792.4÷12k)	232h 42m	1642
SUM (232.7÷24=9.6958)	-228h (9days +12h –{day one})	2842
	004h	-2400
GMT		0442
ZT	(9 days 8/17/99)	-0100
ETA = 9/18/99	0342 ZT	0342

Computing Fuel Requirement:

When loading fuel, *know what you are doing!* A majority of fires and explosions are traceable either to the engine space or the galley. Deviation from established policy or safety regulations causes most accidents.

Since there are no fueling stations in our oceans, careful attention to fuel management is required. You need to know the amount of fuel aboard at all times. Knowledge of fuel inventory is of enormous importance. Not only can a very embarrassing situation develop for a professional mariner but a very dangerous predicament if fuel were unexpectedly depleted. Should fuel consumption appear to be significantly greater than originally estimated an alternate port having appropriate fuel must be considered.

When underway with different cargo weight and with varying fuel consumption rates, along with vessel's underwater condition, fuel management becomes critical. Being a perceptive mariner you may check fuel consumption calculations by comparing fuel consumed on first leg of a voyage to expected mileage on second leg. This ratio of fuel to mileage on first leg to mileage on second leg is solved by cross multiplication and division.

$$\frac{\textbf{MILES FIRST LEG}}{\textbf{FUEL CONSUMED}} \quad \textbf{is to} \quad \frac{\textbf{MILES SECOND LEG}}{\textbf{EXPECTED CNSUMPTION}}$$

EXAMPLE: *On first leg of voyage a ship steamed 201 miles and consumed 18 tons of fuel. What is the expected fuel consumption for 2nd leg of 482 miles?*

$$\frac{201}{18} \quad \text{is to} \quad \frac{482}{x} \quad \text{or} \quad \frac{18 \times 482}{201}$$

$$\frac{8676}{201} = 43.2 \text{ tons}$$

CALCULATOR TI-30Xa

KEY	KEY	DISPLAY	FUNCTION
18	X	18	Fuel consumed 1st leg
482	=	8676	Multiplied by miles 2nd leg
÷	201	201	Divide by fuel 1st leg
=		43.1641791	Expected fuel consumption

Computing Vessel's Propeller Slippage:

Construction of a speed table by engine revolutions should include the consideration of propeller slippage. The number of turns a propeller shaft is proportional to the distance traveled. If the element of time is considered, speed may be determined. In the theoretical situation where a screw propeller is advanced through a solid substance, the distance the screw would advance in one revolution would be equal to the pitch or angle of the propeller blades. Thus, if a propeller having a pitch of ten feet turns at 2,000 revolutions per minute, it would advance 20,000 feet in one minute. This 20,000-foot advance per minute is equivalent to a speed of 19.75 knots.

However, it does not work that easily, because in water we have slip. Slip is the difference between the distance it would advance in a solid substance and actual distance traveled, expressed as a percentage of the former. For example, if slip is 18%, both the ship's speed and distance covered are reduced by this percentage. Instead of 19.7 knots, the speed is only 16.2 knots (19.75 x 0.82).

Slip is determined by comparing the calculated theoretical advance of the propeller to actual experienced performance by the vessel. Slip is expressed as either positive or negative. If the theoretical advance is greater than the performance then the slip is considered positive and 1.0, plus slip percentage is multiplied by speed. But if the theoretical advance is less than the vessel's performance then the slip is considered negative and 1.0, minus slip percentage is multiplied by speed.

To elucidate, revolutions per hour multiplied by propeller pitch, divided by feet in a mile equals theoretical speed. Divide distance traveled by time resulting in actual speed. Now we can make the comparison, divide theoretical speed by actual speed to find the slip. The equation is expressed below:

$$\frac{(\text{Propeller RPM} \times 60 \text{ minutes}) \times \text{pitch}}{6076 \text{ feet (1 nautical mile)}} \div \frac{\text{miles traveled}}{\text{time of travel}} = \text{SLIP}$$

EXAMPLE: *What is the apparent slip if vessel cruised 395 miles in 23 hours, the experienced performance; at average RPM of 78-propeller pitch is 21.6 feet?*

$$\frac{(78 \times 60) \, 21.6}{6076} \div \frac{395}{23} = \text{SLIP}$$

Wilhelm's School Of Navigation

$$\frac{16.63726136}{17.17391304} = 0.968751927 - 1 = 0.0311248073 \text{ OR } 3.1\%$$

The same problem used as an example may be performed on the Texas Instrument calculator TI-30Xa. Following are the keystrokes to solve the same problem:

KEY	KEY	DISPLAY	FUNCTION
78	X	78.	Multiply shaft revolutions (RPM)
60	=	4680	Multiply minutes per hour
X	21.6	21.6	Multiply by propeller pitch
÷	6076	6076	Divide by feet within one mile
=		16.63726136	Theoretical speed
÷	(	16.63726136	Divide and bracket actual speed computation
395	÷	395	Actual distance traveled
23	)	17.17391304	Experienced speed for voyage
=		0.968751927	Result is negative
-	1.0	1.0	
=		-0.031248073	Slippage of 3.1%

EXAMPLE: *We can examine a problem, which has positive slip. The submarine Sea Poacher SS406 has a screw with a diameter of 21.2, pitch 20 feet. What is apparent slip if the Sea Poacher cruises for 391 miles in a 24-hour day at RPM of 88?*

KEY	KEY	DISPLAY	FUNCTION
88	X	88.	Multiply shaft revolutions
60	X	5280	Multiply minutes per hour
X	20	20.	Multiply by propeller pitch
÷	6076	6076	Divide by feet within one mile
=		17.37985517	Theoretical speed
÷	(	0.	Divide and bracket actual speed computation
391	÷	391	Actual distance traveled
24	)	16.29166667	Actual speed
=		1.066794179	Result is positive
-	1.0	1.0	
=		0.066794179	Slippage of + 06.7%

The slippage is plus since the result was a positive one (1.), as opposed to negative result, which a zero prior to the decimal point. Remember theoretical speed divided by actual speed experienced equals slippage.

Wilhelm's School Of Navigation

Required RPM When Slip is known:

A problem occurs when your vessel is scheduled to arrive at a port on a particular day at a designated time. Your shipping agent expects accuracy. The problem is: what engine RPM do we request from the Chief Engineer to obtain the desired speed? First divide the distance by time required to arrive on a particular day at the designated time. This result is the computed speed. When propeller pitch and slip are known, the shaft RPM can be calculated for the required speed.

Steps required solving problem:
1. Number of feet in one mile (6076)
2. Multiplied by required speed
3. Multiply by (1.0 - slip in decimal)
4. Divide by 60 minutes
5. Divide by propeller pitch

EQUATION:
(Positive slip 1.0 + % x speed)
(Negative slip 1.0 - % x speed)

$$\frac{6076 \times (\text{speed} \times \text{slip in decimal})}{60 \text{ minutes} \times \text{propeller pitch}} = \text{SHAFT RPM}$$

EXAMPLE: *The Second Mate computes vessel's speed at 16.3 knots to reach the designated port on time. How many RPM are necessary to obtain the required speed when propeller pitch is 21.7 with a 4% negative slip?*

$$\frac{6076 \times [16.3 \times (1.0-.04)]}{60 \text{ minutes} \times 21.7} = \text{RPM} \qquad \frac{95077.2}{1302} = 73.0$$

TI-30Xa Calculator

KEY	KEY	DISPLAY	FUNCTION
6076	X	6076	Multiply feet per mile
16.3	X	99038.8	Multiply speed
0.96	=	95077.248	Decimal slip (1.0 – 0.04) = 96%
÷	(	0.	Dividing by quotation marks
60	X	60.	Minutes
21.7	)	1302	Divisor
=		73.024	RPM 73 0

Measuring Distance on a Chart:

Distance on charts is measured in nautical miles, (6076 feet), with the exception of Inland Waterway charts, and Great Lakes charts. The Army Corp of Engineers controls the ICW and use statute miles 5,280 feet. Generally most navigators express distance that is less than one mile, in yards. There is approximately 2,025 yards in one mile, and by custom most navigators use 2,000 yard to a mile. However with today's calculators the exact number of 2025.3333 can be used.

Wilhelm's School Of Navigation

Some foreign charts use meters which can be converted 1 meter = 1.09361330 yards, 3.28083990 feet or 0.00053996 of a nautical miles. One nautical mile equals 1,852 meters.

The length of a rhumb line on a chart is measured in nautical mile on the latitude scale at each side of a chart. One nautical mile equals one minute of latitude. There is approximately a tenth of a mile difference when distance is computed mathematically and compared with a rhumb line measurement. Since latitude scale on Mercator charts expand with increasing latitude, measurement should be made at approximately the mid latitude.

Measurement of rhumb line distances on a Mercator projection may be accomplished with a Weems & Plath parallel plotter or with dividers. When the distance to be measured exceeds the divider length, set divider to some convenient distance, a whole number of miles, and then step off necessary number of times, measuring the odd remainder on latitude scale.

The following equation may be used for any distance. Find the great circle distance from Jacksonville Florida 30°19'N, 081°30'W, to North Rock Light, Bermuda 32°28'N, 064°46'W.

$$\text{Departure Latitude} = dL(1)$$
$$\text{Destination Latitude} = dL(2)$$
$$\text{Difference in Longitude} = dL(3)$$

$$\text{Sin } dL(1) \times \text{Sin } dL(2) + \text{Cosin } dL(1) \times \text{Cosin } dL(2) \times \text{Cosin } dL(3) = [\text{Inv}] \times 60 = \text{Distance}$$
$$[\cos]$$

Texas Instrument TI-30Xa			
KEY	KEY	DISPLAY	FUNCTION
30.19	2nd DMS-DD	30.31666667	Minutes to decimal.
STO	1	30.31666667	Store in memory
32.28	2nd DMS-DD	32.46666667	Minutes to decimal
STO	2	32.46666667	Store in memory
16.44	2nd DMS-DD	16.73333333	Minutes to decimal
STO	3	16.73333333	Store in memory
RCL	1	30.31666667	Recall memory
SIN	X	0.504779754	Multiply by sin
RCL	2	32.46666667	Recall memory
SIN	+	0.270969704	Add
RCL	1	30.31666667	Recall memory
COS	X	0.863248753	Multiply by cosin
RCL	2	32.46666667	Recall memory
COS	X	0.728326332	Multiply by cosin
RCL	3	16.73333333	Recall memory
COS	=	0.968455169	Equals
2nd	COS	14.42945876	Invert Cosin
X	60	60	Multiply by 60
=		865.7675253	Distance 865.7 Miles

Wilhelm's School Of Navigation

Great-Circle Sailing:

GREAT CIRCLE DISTANCE, TRUE COURSE FORMULA:

Departure Latitude = dL(1)
Destination Latitude = dL(2)
Difference in Longitude = dL(3)

Sin dL(1) X Sin dL(2) + Cosin dL(1) X Cosin dL(2) X Cosin dL(3) = [Inv] X 60 = Distance
                                                                    [cos]

$$\frac{\text{Sin dL(2)} - \text{Cosin dL(3) X Sin dL(1)}}{\text{Sin dL(3)} \ \& \ \text{Cosin dL(1)}} = \text{[Inv] result is true course or less } 360° \text{ if west}$$
                                                              [cos]

EXAMPLE: Find the great circle distance and true course from, Jacksonville Florida 30°19'N, 081°30'W to North Rock Light, Bermuda 32°28'N, 064°46'W.

Texas Instrument TI-30Xa			
KEY	KEY	DISPLAY	FUNCTION
30.19	2nd DMS-DD	30.31666667	Minutes to decimal.
STO	1	30.31666667	Store in memory
32.28	2nd DMS-DD	32.46666667	Minutes to decimal
STO	2	32.46666667	Store in memory
16.44	2nd DMS-DD	16.73333333	Minutes to decimal
STO	3	16.73333333	Store in memory
RCL	1	30.31666667	Recall memory
SIN	X	0.504779754	Multiply by sin
RCL	2	32.46666667	Recall memory
SIN	+	0.270969704	Add
RCL	1	30.31666667	Recall memory
COS	X	0.863248753	Multiply by cosin
RCL	2	32.46666667	Recall memory
COS	X	0.728326332	Multiply by cosin
RCL	3	16.73333333	Recall memory
COS	=	0.968455169	Equals
2nd	COS	14.42945876	Invert Cosin
STO	3	14.42945876	Minutes to decimal.
X	60	60	Multiply by 60
=		865.7675253	Distance 865.7 Miles
RCL	2	32.46666667	Recall memory
SIN	-	0.536808852	Subtract
RCL	3	14.42945876	Recall memory
COS	X	0.968455169	Multiply by Sin
RCL	1	30.316666667	Recall memory
SIN	=	0.047953259	Equals
÷		0.047953259	Divide
RCL	3	14.42945876	Recall memory
SIN	÷	0.192438187	Divide
RCL	1	30.31666667	Recall memory
COS	=	0.2229233215	Equal
2nd	COS	77.11921428	True Course 077°

Wilhelm's School Of Navigation

Great-circle sailing employs the solution for a series of various rhumb lines contributing to a line traced on the surface of a sphere by a plane that cuts through the sphere center. A great circle is the largest circle that can be drawn on the surface of the sphere, and is the shortest distance between any two points on the earth's surface. Meridians of longitude, and the equator are great circles. By steering a series of rhumb lines a ship can maintain a constant true course following a great-circle track.

A solution for a great-circle track can be computed providing shortest distance and true course to point of greatest latitude called the **vertex.** The Great Circle course is continuously changing. Customarily no exact attempt is made to follow exactly but a series of rhumb lines are used to approximate the Great Circle course.

Plane Sailing:

The area of the earth where a voyage is planned is considered a plane or flat surface in regard to plane sailing. Only course and distance, difference of latitude, and departure are measured. The meridian through the point of departure, the parallel through the point of arrival, and the course line form a right triangle. Plane sailing should not be used for any distances over 200 miles. The following equations will solve for the difference in latitude through departure point to parallel of latitude.

Difference of latitude $= \text{Distance} \times \cos \text{Course}$
Distance East or West of departure $= \text{Distance} \times \sin \text{Course}$

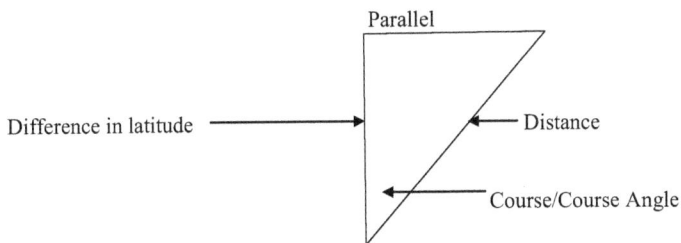

EXAMPLES: *A vessel steams 188.4 miles on a true course of 005°. What is the difference in latitude, and parallel of latitude?*

1. $188.4 \times \cos 005 = 187.7$'N difference in latitude
2. $188.4 \times \sin 005 = 16.4$ mi. E parallel of latitude

Wilhelm's School Of Navigation

A ship has steamed 136.6 miles north and 203.1 miles west. What is the Distance and course?

$$\text{Parallel} = 203.1$$
$$\text{Difference in Latitude} = 136.6 \text{ miles}$$

1.. $\dfrac{203.1}{136.6} = 1.48682284$ 2nd tan $= 56.07620594$ (2nd DD-DMS)

2. $\quad 360°00.0$
    $\quad \underline{056°04.6}$
    $\quad 303°56.4$ or $303°.9$ course $304°T$

3. $\dfrac{203.1}{\text{Sin } 56.076} = 244.7 \text{ miles}$

Traverse Sailing:

Traverse sailing is computing a single course and distance after a series of course lines. This might result from a sailing vessel tacking into the wind or a search and rescue mission finding most logical search datum. Another situation develops when an estimated current is to be considered, set is treated as an additional course line, and drift is the ratio of distance to time.

The known values in this problem are vessel's course and speed through the water, and vessel's course and speed made good over ground (SMG). Two vectors are known, therefore an equation follows:

$$\text{COURSE - TAN}^{-1} = \frac{\text{SOG X } \sin \text{COG} - \text{Speed X } \sin \text{Course}}{\text{SOG X } \cos \text{COG} - \text{Speed X } \cos \text{Course}}$$

$$\text{SPEED} = \frac{\text{SOG X } \sin \text{COG} - \text{Speed } \sin \text{Course}}{\sin \text{Set}}$$

In situations with several different course and speed changes, the equations are computed for the first two vectors. The resulting vector is used to solve for the next vector and so on until the final composite vector is found. A course must be added or subtracted to 180° or 360° depending upon its quadrant as shown below:

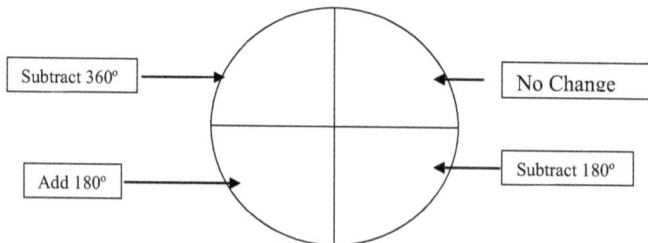

Subtract 360° | No Change

Add 180° | Subtract 180°

Wilhelm's School Of Navigation

EXAMPLE: *Ship steering a course of 255°, speed 12 knots makes good a course of 245°, speed 13.4 knots. What is the third vector's set and drift?*

$$\frac{13.4 \times \sin 245 - 12.0 \times \sin 255}{13.4 \times \cos 245 - 12.0 \times \cos 255} \quad \begin{array}{l} = \text{Inv } 12° + 180° = 192° \\ \tan \end{array}$$

$$\frac{13.4 \times \sin 245 - 12.0 \times \sin 255}{\sin 192} = 2.7 \text{ knots}$$

Parallel Sailing:

Parallel sailing is the *"interconversion"* of departure point and difference of longitude when a vessel proceeds due east or due west. This was a common form of navigation prior to navigators being able to determine longitude. Today it has very little use or need for such computations. Parallel sailing is the simplest form of spherical sailings. The equation follows:

$$\text{Difference in degrees of longitude} = \frac{\text{Distance Run}}{60 \cos \text{Latitude (in decimal degrees)}}$$

EXAMPLE: *A ship in DR latitude 49°40'.2N is on a course of 090°. What is the change in longitude when the vessel has sailed 136.4 miles?*

$$\frac{136.4}{60 (\cos 49.4012)} = \text{Difference in Longitude}$$

$$\frac{136.4}{60 \times 0.647189023} = \text{Difference in Longitude}$$

$$\frac{136.4}{38.83134138} = 3°30'45" \text{ or } 3°30.8E$$

TI-30Xa Calculator

KEY	KEY	DISPLAY	FUNCTION
136.4	STO 1	136.4	Distance STO 1
49.4012	2nd DMS-DD	49.67	Lat. decimal form
COS	X	0.647189023	Cosine, Multiply
60	=	38.83134138	Minutes, Equals
STO 2	RCL 1	136.4	Store memory 2
÷	RCL 2	38.83134138	Divisor
=		3.512626532	Dec. difference
2nd DD-DMS		3°30'45"	3°30.8

Wilhelm's School Of Navigation

Middle-Latitude Sailing:

Mid-latitude sailing combines plane sailing and parallel sailing. Plane sailing is used to find difference of latitude and departure when course and distance are known. Parallel sailing is used to interconvert departure and difference of longitude; middle latitude is used to determine latitude and longitude.

EXAMPLE: *A ship, the American Mariner departs 26°15.0N, 047°15.0W and steams 2h 28m at 21.7k on a true course of 130°. What is latitude and longitude at destination?*

KEY	KEY	DISPLAY	FUNCTION	Mid-Lat.
2.28	2nd DMS-DD	2.466666667	Time in decimal	26°15.0N
X	21.7	21.7	Speed	- 00°34.4S Lat diff
=	2nd x-y	21.7	Polar rectangle	25°40.6N New Lat.
130	2nd P-R	34.40627812	Lat. difference	+ 26°15.0N
2nd x-y	÷	41.00380556	Polar rectangle	51°55.6 ÷ 2
25.5748	2nd DMS-DD	25.96333333	Mid-Lat. cosin	= 25°57.8N Mid-Lat.
COS	=	45.60668792	Lo. Difference	
				047°15.0W
				- 000°45.6E Lo diff
				046°29.4W Lo.

Mercator Sailing:

Mercator sailing is easily solved for relative short distances with a rhumb line graphically drawn on a Mercator chart projection. Otherwise a mathematical solution is available when using Table 6 found in 1995 addition of *American Practical Navigator* authored by Nathaniel Bowditch. This "Table 6" contains the Meridional parts used in the construction of Mercator charts. In addition, Mercator sailing is tabulated to one decimal place for each minute of latitude from equator to the pole.

Mathematical solution for Mercator sailing use the following equations:

$$\frac{\text{Difference in Longitude}}{\text{Meridional parts}} = \text{Inv tan} \quad \text{result is the Angle}$$

$$\frac{\text{Difference in Latitude}}{\cos \text{Angle}} = \text{Distance}$$

EXAMPLE: *A vessel underway from latitude 32°14.7N, longitude 066°28.9W is making to the Chesapeake sea buoy latitude 36°58.7N, longitude 075°42.2W. What is the course and distance?*

Wilhelm's School Of Navigation

	Latitude	Longitude	Meridional
Departure	32°14.7N	066°28.9W	2033.3
Destination	36°58.7N	075°42.2W	2377.0
Diff. of Lat/Lo	04°44.0N	009°13.3W	0343.7
Minutes	284.0N	553.3W	0300.0
			5°43.7

Compute Angle and Course:

Dif. Lo.   09.1318 = Inv N58°09'.1W subtract 360° = 301°.8 C

Meridional Table 6 05.4342   tan

Compute Distance

Dif. Lat. in minutes   284   = 538.2 miles

Angle of Triangle   cos 58.0906

Relative Bearing Of Contact:

A **Relative Bearing** is a direction from an observer to a reported contact measured from the vessel's bow clockwise 360°. Imagine standing in the center of a compass rose and looking straight ahead at 000° / 360°, no matter what the ship's magnetic compass or gyrocompass show, the vessel's bow is always 000° / 360°. Contacts are reported in relation to the bow. A contact broad on starboard beam has relative bearing of 090° while a contact broad on port beam bears 270°. Contacts dead astern are 180° while a contact dead ahead is 000° or 360° regardless of what the ship's compass reads.

Relative bearing may be measured using the ship's pelorus, a dumb compass. It is called a dumb compass because the 360° compass card does not rotate, and north 000° / 360° is always pointed at ship's bow. A few students have a tendency to confuse ships heading and true bearing. Ship heading is always direction vessel is moving while true bearing always refers to the contact or object sighted.

Many problems requiring solution use relative bearings. Also, when it becomes necessary to know the true bearing of a contact, a navigator must be ready to convert relative bearings to true and true bearings to relative. One way to remember the equation that converts these bearings is a name such as *"ReST"*. The word *"ReST"* stands for relative bearing plus ships heading equals true bearing. The equations that convert relative to true, and true to relative are as follows:

Relative Bearing = RB
Ship's Heading = SH
True Bearing   = TB

RB + SH = TB
TB - SH = RB

Wilhelm's School Of Navigation

EXAMPLE: *A vessel on a course 237°T, speed 17k sights Cape Henry Light bearing 050°RB. What is the true bearing of Cape Henry Light?*

$$RB + SH = TB$$
$$050° + 237° = 287°$$

Ship's true course is 237° with Set and Drift reported as 130° at 2.4 knots. To solve for leeway the set of 130° true must be converted to a relative bearing as follows:

$$TB - SH = RB$$
$$130° - 237° = 253°$$

Course to Steer by Leeway & Speed over Ground (SOG):

An external dominant force of wind, sea or a combination thereof affects a course in current. This external force exerts pressure on the bow that retards forward motion or pushes the stern to increase speed. Calculate current affect by subtracting or adding the external force speed to vessel's speed. A majority of the time the current or force has any of a possible 360° influences on the vessel. The relative bearing of the *leeway* is a necessary consideration for a solution.

Before proceeding further, the student needs to understand nautical terms used in this explanation:

    Course - the direction to destination of a vessel used for *dead reckoning*. "C"
    Speed - time taken to travel, 6076 ft. (one nautical mile) in an hour. "S"
    Track - expected path over bottom (true) considering set and drift. "TR"
    Speed of advance – intended rate of travel along intended track. "SOA"
    Course Over Ground – average path traveled "COG" "course made good CMG"
    Speed Over Ground - actual rate of travel accomplished "SMG"
    Vector - mathematical term for a line having magnitude and direction.
    Leeway - number of degrees needed to off set external force of wind or sea.
    Set - direction vessel is being pushed.
    Drift - speed of vessel is being set.

Leeway by definition is the leeward (away from the wind) motion of a vessel because of external force of wind or sea. By considering the wind and sea forces as one force there is no need to consider them separately. The leeward motion of a vessel is the result of two factors, *set* and *drift*. Drift is the speed that a vessel is set (direction of vessel) by these external forces.

The relative bearing of *leeway* is determined by subtracting ship's heading from the true bearing of the external force, *set*. The acronym, (THER) may be helpful in remembering this equation. T stands for *True Bearing* of the set. H stands for ship's heading or the intended course. E is to remind you of equals, and R stands for *relative bearing* of the set. To illustrate:

EXAMPLE: *The Gulf Stream runs north at and average speed of 2.5 knots. What is the relative bearing of the Gulf Stream on a vessel steaming a course of 090°?*

Wilhelm's School Of Navigation

$$\frac{TB \quad\quad SH \quad\quad RB}{360° - 090° = 270°}$$

When solving a current problem calculate leeway, which is the result of set and drift. This may be accomplished either of two ways, Texas Instrument calculator TI30Xa, or by a vector diagram. When solving with a vector diagram:

1. Draw a vector diagram with course vector the length in units of speed from center of a Maneuvering Board or Compass Rose in degrees of direction intended.

2. From center of diagram draw length of set vector, (current vector) in units of speed in degrees in direction of leeward motion.

3. Set dividers for vessel's speed, place left point at end of current vector and swing an arc across course vector.

4. A line from end of current vector and arc point represents heading necessary to make intended track, course to steer.

5. To read correct heading walk line with parallel ruler, parallel to center of compass rose and where line crosses compass rose read degrees. Difference between "B" and "F" is your leeway.

6. The difference between course line and parallel line is the leeway.

7. SOG is equal to vector AD

Maneuvering Board solution

True Course 237° Speed 17 knots

Set & Drift 130° 2.4 knots

Course Line   = AB
Ships Vector = AC
Set Vector   = AD
Result Vector = DE
Course to Steer = AF

Wilhelm's School Of Navigation

bearing while set is in direction of movement. Leeway customarily is used to describe the affect of dominant force be it current, wind, or geographical error.

When a mandatory voyage plan is constructed, an estimate of the effect of the current on the desired track is essential. A solution for **course over ground (COG)**, and **speed over ground (SOG)** may be computed with an equation or graphically.

Solving a current problem using a Texas Instrument calculator, TI30Xa, the relative bearing of the set is computed first, and entered into the following equation:

D   = drift
RBS   = relative bearing of set
S   = vessel's speed

$$Leeway = sin^{-1} \frac{D \times sin\ RBS}{S}$$

$$SOG = (cosin\ Leeway \times S) + (D \times cosin\ RBS)$$

EXAMPLE: *The bulk carrier Global Star plans a voyage from Fort Pierce Florida to Freeport Grand Bahama Island on a true course of 105°, speed 12 knots, variation 5°W, and deviation 2°E. Expected set and drift crossing Gulf Stream is north at 3 knots. What is the course to steer and SOG?*

TB - SH = RB
360° - 105° = 255°

$$\frac{3 \times sin\ 255°}{12} = (2^{nd}sin)\ is\ -14°$$

$$(cos\ 13.97399363 \times 12) + (3 \times cos\ 255°) = 10.9k$$

KEY	KEY	DISPLAY	FUNCTION
3	X	3	Enter Drift 3K, and multiplied
255	SIN	-0.965925826	Set 255 Sin
=	÷	-2.897777479	Equal and Divide
12	=	-0.241481457	Vessel speed, Equals
2ⁿᵈ	SIN	-13.97399363	Result is Leeway 14°
COS	X	0.970405434	Cosine leeway, and multiply
12	=	11.64486521	Vessel speed, and equal
+	3	3	Add, and enter Drift
X	255	255	Multiply, and enter Set
CO3	=	10.86840807	Cosine, and equal SOG 10.9K

TC L   COG V   MC D   CC
105 +14 119 5W 124 2E 122

EXAMPLE: *Vessel's Master approves a voyage plan for a true course of 265°, and a speed of 15 knots through a current having a set of 185° / drift 3 knots. What is the course to steer and speed over ground?*

Wilhelm's School Of Navigation

$$\frac{3 \times \sin(185 - 265)}{15} = \text{Inv} \ \text{Result} \ 11.35933475 \ \text{or} \ 11° + 265° = 276°$$

$$(\sin 11.35933475 \times 15) + (3 \times \sin 280) = 15.22711274 \ \text{or} \ 15.2 \ \text{knots}$$

Current Sailing-Finding Set and Drift:

Set and drift or current sailing can be found after a course and speed made good vector has been created from a fixed position. Subtracting the CMG vector from the Course vector results in the set vector. A personal calculator will quickly compute set and drift. Rather than using the graphic technique, which is not as accurate, subtracting two vectors by calculator will achieve a more accurate result. This procedure is the resolution of two vectors into their north-south and east-west components, the subtraction of these components, and the establishment of a third vector establishes set and drift.

Our method for solving for set and drift develops a *"course steered vector"*, and *"speed of advance over a desired track vector"*. Subtracting these two vectors, the *"current vector"* is revealed.

Path over ground   -   Path thru water   =   Current

EQUATION:

$$\frac{(\text{Speed} \times \sin \text{COG}) - (\text{Speed} \times \sin \text{TC})}{(\text{Speed} \times \cos \text{COG}) - (\text{Speed} \times \cos \text{TC})} \quad \begin{array}{l} \text{Inv} = \text{SET} \\ \tan \end{array}$$

$$\frac{(\text{Speed} \times \sin \text{Course}) + (\text{Drift} \times \sin \text{Set})}{\sin \text{SET}} = \text{DRIFT}$$

EXAMPLE: *Vessel's Master approves a voyage plan for a course of 255°T, and a speed of 12 knots through a current that result in course over ground (COG) of 245° with a 13-knot speed made good (SMG). What is the set and drift experienced?*

$$\frac{(12 \times \sin 255) - (13 \times \sin 185)}{(12 \times \cos 255) - (13 \times \cos 185)} \quad \begin{array}{l} \text{Inv} = 12° + 180° = 192° \\ \tan \end{array}$$

To find direction, establish quadrant:

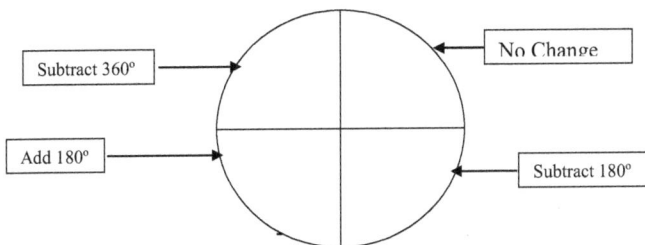

Subtract 360°

Add 180°

No Change

Subtract 180°

Wilhelm's School Of Navigation

Computation for Drift:

$$\frac{(12 \times \sin 255) - (13 \times \sin 185)}{\sin 192°} = 2.617 \text{ or } 2.6 \text{ of Drift}$$

Current Sailing-Finding Course to Steer and Speed Vector:

Establishing a vessel's estimated position after traveling a selected track that has been degraded by external forces may be solved using vectors. Two known values are used, (1) set and drift, and (2) Vessel's speed through the water (S) and direction of the track along which it desired to sail. To acquire the course to be steered and speed of advance the following equation provides a solution.

EQUATION:

$$\frac{\text{Drift} \times \sin \text{(Relative Bearing of Set)}}{\text{Vessel's Speed}} = \frac{\text{Inv}}{\text{Sin}} = \text{Leeway} +/- \text{ Track} = \text{Course to steer}$$

$$(\cos \text{Leeway} \times \text{Vessel's Speed}) + (\text{Drift} \times \cos \text{Set}) = \text{Speed of Advance}$$

EXAMPLE: *The 2nd mate aboard the vessel American Pride develops a voyage plan to its current destination, a course of 080° true, at a speed 10 knots. The set and drift along the intended track is estimated at drift 4 knots, and set of 140°. The problem is what course should the American Pride steer in order to make good the intended track? To develop an estimated arrival time (ETA) the speed of advance (SOA) needs to be solved.*

$$\frac{4 \times \sin (140° - 080°)}{10 \text{ knots}} = \frac{\text{Inv}}{\text{Sin}} \quad 20.3 - 080° = 060° \text{ course to steer}$$

$$(\cos 20.3 \times 10k) + (4 \times \cos 060) = 11.4 \text{ knots SOA}$$

Current Sailing-Finding COG & SOG

In a situation where the set and drift are known or with a reasonable estimate the course over ground (COG), and speed over ground (SOG) can be calculated. This circumstances results by adding two vectors to obtain (COG).

$$\overrightarrow{\text{Path over ground}} = \overrightarrow{\text{Path thru water}} + \overrightarrow{\text{Current}}$$

EQUATION:

Course Over Ground:

$$\frac{(\text{Vessel's Speed} \times \sin \text{Course}) + (\text{Drift} \times \sin \text{Set})}{(\text{Vessel's Speed} \times \cos \text{Course}) + (\text{Drift} \times \cos \text{Set})} = \text{COG}$$

Speed Over Ground:

Wilhelm's School Of Navigation

$$\frac{\text{(Vessel's Speed x }_{\sin}\text{Course)} + \text{(Drift x }_{\sin}\text{Set}}{_{\sin}\text{COG}} = \text{SOG}$$

EXAMPLE: *The motor vessel Symphony underway on a course of 070° true, speed 10 knots encounters a set of 130° with a drift of 3 knots. What is the course over ground (COG) and speed over ground (SOG)?*

Course Over Ground:

$$\frac{(10 \text{ x }_{\sin}070) + (3 \text{ x }_{\sin}130)}{(10 \text{ x }_{\cos}070) + (3 \text{ x }_{\cos}130)} = \frac{\text{Inv}}{\tan} = 82.73052779 \text{ or } 83° \text{ course over ground}$$

Speed Over Ground:

$$\frac{(10 \text{ x }_{\sin}070) + (3 \text{ x }_{\sin}130)}{_{\sin}83°} = 11.78288739 \text{ or } 11.8 \text{ knots}$$

Estimate Position With One LOP:

Competent navigators maintain a constant dead reckoning plot, plotting the vessel's dead reckoning position (DR) at least every hour when located in coastal waters. A situation where dangers to navigation are of concern, and the navigator feels that time is of the essence; an estimated position may be required when waiting a second bearing for a running fix.

An estimated position can be obtained from a single LOP. Establish a DR position, using the same time as the line of position (LOP). Draw a line from the DR position that matches the time of the LOP intersecting the LOP at a right angle (90°). Where this line intersects the LOP is the estimated position (EP). However, when a beam bearing is plotted so that the LOP intersects the DR track at a right angle (90°) the estimated position (EP) is located at that intersection.

Wilhelm's School Of Navigation

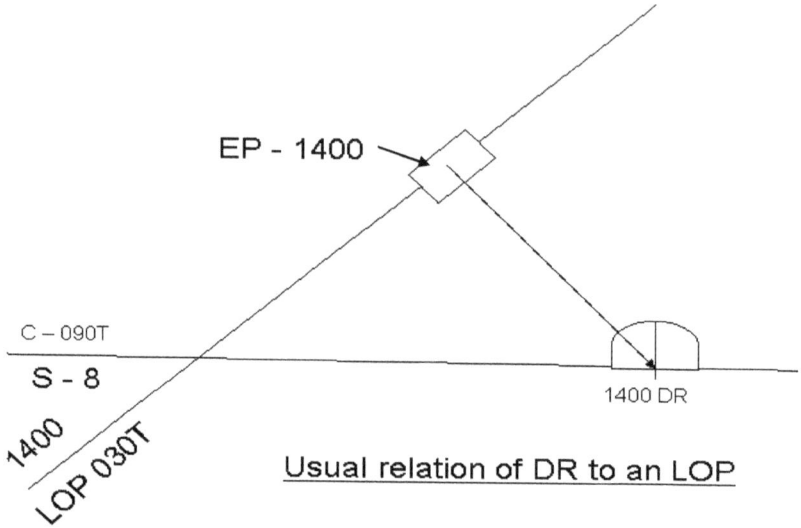

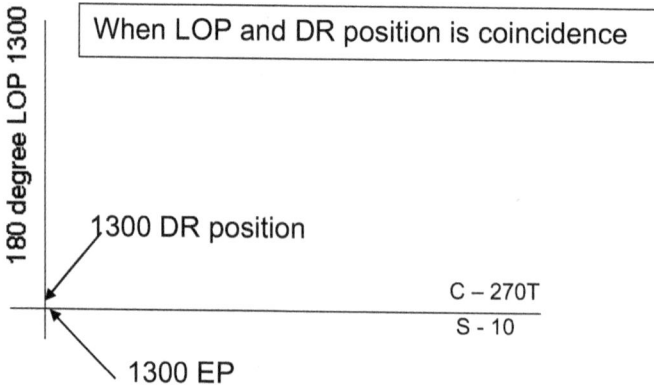

EP - 1400

C – 090T

S - 8

1400

LOP 030T

1400 DR

Usual relation of DR to an LOP

180 degree LOP 1300

When LOP and DR position is coincidence

1300 DR position

C – 270T

S - 10

1300 EP

Position by Two or More Lines of Position (LOP):

The fundamental elements of establishing a position are two or more lines of position. The usual method to establish a fix, as in fix your position, are accomplished by crossing two or more lines of position. Obviously the observer's location is at the intersection of these two or more Lops. With only one LOP the observer knows he is somewhere along the line of position but has no means of determining location along this line.

All lines of position drawn on a chart must be labeled immediately. This label should indicate the bearing written below the line, with time of bearing written above in what is referred to as military time. To minimize any inaccuracy of a fix with only two line of position, the angle of intersection should be as close to 90° as possible. An optimum fix would include three or more lines of position taken simultaneously. The angle of intersection for three lines would be as close to 120° apart as possible.

Three lines of position will usually form a small triangle, referred to as "*cocked hat*". It is customary to use the center of the small triangle as the selected probable position. In a three line or more fix one or more bearing lines may not be consistent with the other bearing lines; this obvious error may be discarded or new round bearings may be repeated. Any obvious significant error with any one of the Lops, the navigator must check calculations and plotting technique.

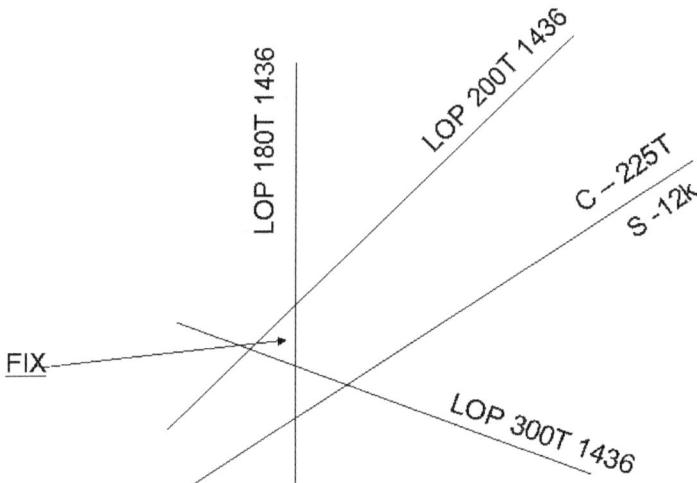

A fix is plotted on a chart as a small circle with a dot at the center. Label the fix with the time. When passing close aboard to an ATON within a boat length or so, the ATON is considered the fix and so labeled. With any distance greater, an estimate is made and plotted accordingly.

Position by Two Radar Ranges:

Wilhelm's School Of Navigation

Radar has the ability to establish a fix when there is little or no visibility. In addition, considerable distance is available as opposed to eyesight. But radar has a problem with bearings. A radar bearing is not reliable because many radar antennas may not be aligned with the vessel's keel. Furthermore, the transmitted electronic pulse by a radar unit increases in width the further the range. This distorts the bearing of the returning echo.

A radar range is usually more accurate than a radar bearing. Obtaining a fix by two or more ranges is generally preferable to one obtained by two bearings or by a range and bearing. However, an accurate range requires reliable identification of the contacts returning the echo. A visual fix, weather conditions permitting, is more reliable than two radar ranges taken simultaneously.

Identify two or more contacts that will produce a good returning echo. Set radar range scale to appropriate range. Sight navigational contact on the PPI scope (plan position indicator) setting range marker on target. Run out the adjustable ring synchronized with the range counter and read range to target. Another method of measuring range by radar is to use the series of visible concentric circles at established distances from the center. The concentric circles probably will not produce the accuracy of a range counter unless a ring accidentally falls over a targeted aid.

Bearing and Distance Off AT 2nd LOP (Running Fix):

When a second navigational aid is not available for a second **line of position** (**LOP**) some method of determining ship location is necessary to avoid dangers to navigation. In such a situation it becomes essential for navigators to avail themselves of a somewhat less accurate **running fix**. A running fix is only as good as the accuracy of the vessel's speed and course. The time run interval should be minimum. For coastal piloting keep the time run to approximately 30 or 45 minutes. Longer time intervals cause more uncertainty.

CHART METHOD FOR ADVANCING ONE LOP:
1. Observe a bearing on ATON noting the time of observation and speed.
2. Wait approximately 30 minutes and take a second observation.
3. Calculate distance run = (Speed x Time Run).
4. Advance ATON observed in direction of course line the distance run.
5. Draw 1st LOP from the point of the advanced ATON.
6. Draw 2nd LOP from the point on chart of ATON observed,
7. At the intersection of the two Lops is vessels fix position
8. Label bearing and time of each LOP, and Time of fix.

EQUATION:
$$\frac{\text{Distance Run x } \sin 1^{st} \text{ relative bearing}}{\sin(1^{st} \text{ relative bearing} - 2^{nd} \text{ relative bearing})} = \text{Distance off at } 2^{nd} \text{ LOP}$$

Wilhelm's School Of Navigation

EXAMPLE: *While the war ship Missouri was steaming on a true course of 360° at 18 knots the ship executive officer observes Fowey Rocks Light at 1423 bearing 335° relative. Again at 1455 the same light bears 305° relative. What is the distance off at 1455?*

$$\frac{9.6 \text{ X sin} 335}{\text{Sin } 30} = 8.1 \text{M Distance off } 2^{nd} \text{ LOP}$$

The following table presentation shows the TI-30Xa calculator steps necessary to solve for distance off at 2nd bearing and for distance off when abeam. Note: the P-R key provides distance to abeam which may be required for an ETA.

CALCULATOR TI-30Xa:

KEY	KEY	DISPLAY	FUNCTION
14.55	2nd DMS-DD	14.91666667	Time 2nd LOP
-	14.23	14.38333333	Subtract 1st LOP
2nd DMS-DD	=	0.53333333	32 minutes traveled
X	18	18	Multiply by speed
=	STO 1	9.60000001	Distance traveled
X	335	335	Multiply by 1st LOP
SIN	=	-4.057135313	Result multiplication
÷	30	30	Difference between Lops
SIN	=	8.114270625	Answer 8.1 Miles
2nd x-y	305	305	2nd relative bearing
2nd P-R		-4.6541554429	Distance to abeam
2nd x-y		-4.654154429	Distance off abeam

The small size and the light weight of personal calculators make them a suitable navigation tool. I have found the Texas Instrument TI-30Xa inexpensive and exceptionally reliable. Calculators are especially applicable aboard small ships, those under 50 tons, where a chart room is nonexistent and plotting become a problem. Maintaining a navigation log solves this problem.

Position by Bearing &Angle:

A fix can be obtained from a single observed bearing with angle on a solitary aid to navigation. Quite often on coastal passage only a single navigational aid is within sight at any one time. Fortunately the navigator has the opportunity to surmount this problem with a sextant angle. Simply observe the bearing and

Wilhelm's School Of Navigation

height of the navigational aid, such as a lighthouse, correcting for the height of observer's eye.

Using your calculator you can easily divide the published height by tangent (TAN) of the observed angle. The resulting answer is in feet, when height is entered in feet, and the number of feet may so large to be meaningless. Overcomes this by dividing the answer by 6,076, the number of feet within a nautical Mile. As you can see the answer is in miles and tenths of a mile, easily comprehend able.

However, sextants will develop an error over time because of mirror adjustments. Prior to taking the observed height, place the index arm on zero. Looking at the horizon, adjusting the arc until the horizon is a straight line. Read the amount of difference, if below zero on the arc, add, and if above zero, subtract. Simple saying, *off is on*, add, and *on is off*, subtract. Also, the sextant arc reading will be in degrees, minutes and tenth, and the minutes and tenth must be converted into decimal format.

EQUATION:

$$\frac{\text{Height of Structure}}{\text{tan Angle}} = \text{Distance to structure}$$

EXAMPLE: *The sailing vessel Bermuda High observes with a sextant having and index error of .02 off the arc, dip is .8, "Buzzard Light" 101 feet high, bearing 330°T, with a sextant height of 15.9.*

Height by sextant	15.9
Sextant error	+00.2
Height of eye	-00.8
Apparent Height	15.3 2nd DMS-DD or 0.255

$$\frac{101}{\text{tan } 0.255} = 22693.47 \div 6076 = 3.7 \text{ miles}$$

TI-30Xa Calculator

KEY	KEY	DISPLAY	FUNCTION
101	÷	101	Enter height of Buzzard light
.1518	2nd DMS-DD	0.255	Change minutes to decimal
TAN	=	22693.47264	Tangent, Equal
÷	6076	6076	Number of feet in a mile
=		3.734963247	Distance to Buzzard light

Passing Buoy Predetermined Distance from Afar:

Wilhelm's School Of Navigation

From a fix a vessel needs to change its course to avoid a navigational hazard or to pass an *ATON* a certain distance off. First question, what is the new course to avoid the obstruction passing at a predetermined distance, and the second question is what time will this vessel clear the obstruction or hazard. Method solution using equations:

$$\frac{\text{Distance Off}}{\text{Distance To Go}} = \text{Inv Sin} \quad \text{Result is the Angle}$$

$$\frac{\text{Distance Off}}{\text{Tan Angle}} = \text{Distance to go (DTG)}$$

$$\frac{\text{Distance to Go}}{\text{Speed}} = \text{Time to Go (TTG)}$$

METHOD:

✓ DETERMINE ANGLE TO WAYPOINT (DOF ÷ DTG; Inv Sin = ANGLE)
✓ DISTANCE OFF (DOF) ÷ tan ANGLE – Dist. to go (DTG)
✓ DISTANCE TO GO ÷ SPEED = TIME TO GO

EXAMPLE: *The motor vessel, Port Deposit, is making a speed of 6k, a navigational mark observed 10NM ahead at 0900, the vessel changes its course to pass mark 5 NM off. What is the course and ETA?*

DOF	DTG	RESULT
5 NM	10	= 2nd SIN Result is 30 °
5 NM	30 tan	8.7 NM is the distance to go
8.7 NM	6k	1h 27m is the time to go
1h 27m	0900	1027

CALCULATOR KEY STROKES TI-30Xa:

KEY	KEY	DISPLAY	FUNCTION
5	STO 1	5	Distance off
÷	10	10	Result if division
=	2nd SIN	30	Angle
STO	2	30	Store in memory 1
RCL 1	÷	5	Distance off
RCL 2	TAN	0.577350269	Tangent angle
=	STO 3	8.660254038	Distance to go (DTG)
RCL 3	÷		Recall memory 3
6	=	1.443375673	Time to go in decimal form
÷	09.00	9.00	Time of observation
2nd DMS-DD	=	10.44337567	Change to decimal
2nd DD-DMS		10° 26'36"1	10h 26m 30s

Wilhelm's School Of Navigation

EXAMPLE: *While on a course of 180° Pgc, an anchored vessel bears 1° on the port bow at a radar range of 8 miles. What course should you steer to pass ½ mile off to port?*

.5 ÷ $\tan 8 = 4°$ angle

Course	180°
Angle on bow	001°
Bearing to obstruction	179°
Angle correction	004°
New Course	183°

Danger Bearings and Angles:

Observing only a single line of position may seem like half a loaf to many navigators, but one line of position can be most reassuring. One line of position establishes the fact that the vessel is somewhere along that track. In many situations there are dangers to navigation that must be avoided. A single bearing line can determine when danger is eminent.

It may be because of inattention of the helmsman or due to leeway or some other reason but the navigator needs some assurance to know when vessel's course is not proceeding in a straight line. The vessel is slowly carried off its DR track to one side, and into the possibility of a dangerous situation.

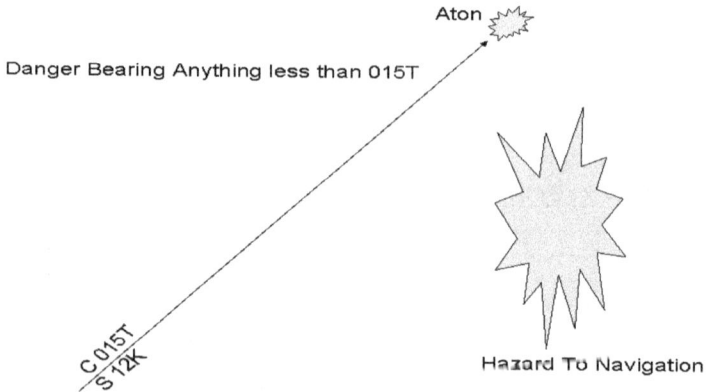

Aton

Danger Bearing Anything less than 015T

C 015T
S 12K

Hazard To Navigation

Another use for danger bearings is the establishment of a danger area by using a danger angle. When an aid to navigation or some other prominent feature is visible, a danger bearing can be established with a bearing line from the aid to navigation, tangent to the danger.

Wilhelm's School Of Navigation

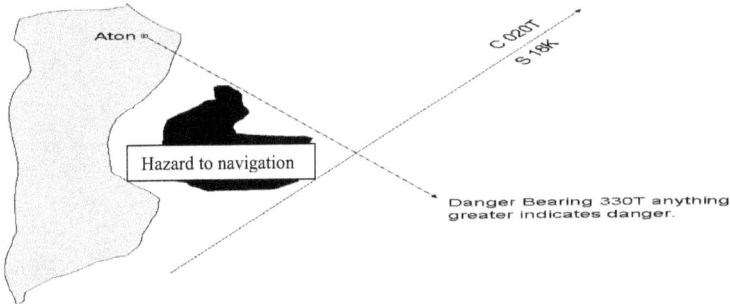

Danger Bearing 330T anything greater indicates danger.

As the vessel approaches the hazardous area, the navigator observes a series of bearings, and depending on vessel's compass course the bearings will increase or decrease indicating numerically whether the vessel is steaming into area of danger. To illustrate, while steaming on a course of 360° true, you establish a danger bearing of (not more than) NMT 315° true. This means that any observation more than 315° could be critical as opposed to any bearing less than 315°. If the vessel were off course to the west, the bearing would be more than 315°.

Horizontal Danger Angles:

A horizontal angle measured between two identifiable fixed aids to navigation defines a circle of position. An angle between any two aids to navigation located on the circumference of a circle, which intersects two aids to navigation will be the same at any location on that circumference. Therefore, we know, for example, that when a danger to navigation lies inshore of our course line it can be avoided because this danger to navigation lies within the circle of position. Since any angle measured between two aids will be the same anywhere on that circle.

To determine a danger angle, a circle must be established to indicate the boundary between a position of safety and those of possible danger. By drawing a circle around a danger to navigation that intersects two aids to navigation, and then measuring the angle between, we can stay clear when the angle measured is less than the danger angle. The further away the lesser the angle, and conversely when closer the greater the angle.

Anywhere inside the circle of position the angle is larger and anywhere outside this circle it is smaller. When a vessel is to pass between a danger to navigation, and two aids to navigation forming a circle of position, anywhere outside the circle indicates jeopardy. Therefore a minimum horizontal danger angle is used when a vessel is to pass inside an off-lying danger to navigation. The minimum danger angle is effective only while the vessel is inside the circle. To be outside the circle of position places the vessel in the hazard area.

Wilhelm's School Of Navigation

Danger Angle anything less than 36 °

Tide Height Calculation:

Procedure and instruction for height of tide at desired time using tide publication:

1. Enter Table 2 – *Tidal Differences And Other Constants*
   a. Look up "PLACE" - Harbor of interest where water height is required
   b. Extract (1) time and (2) water differences plus (3) reference station
   c. Make note of these three enumerates on your worksheet (see work form next page)
2. Enter Table 1 – *Daily Tide Predictions*
   a. Look up reference station page with date of inquiry.
   b. Note time of high to low or low to high that straddles desired time.
   c. Extract the time of high and low, plus water height in feet that straddles desired time.
   d. Make note of these enumerates on your worksheet.

3. Correct Time and Water Height Differences Extracted From TABLE 1
   a. Add / subtract as indicated the time difference taken from Table 2.
   b. Add / subtract or multiply water height differences taken from Table 2.
   c. Correct using algebraic signs – (" * " asterisk denotes multiply)
   d. Enter enumerates on WORK FORM

4. Compute "*DURATION*" by subtracting. That is the difference between the time of high and low water establishes the duration of the rise or fall.
5. Compute "*TIME OF NEAREST TIDE*", which is the time difference between desired times and closest high or low water. In other words, the least or smallest time from desired time to high or between desired time and low water.
6. Compute "*RANGE*", which is the difference in feet between the high and low water that straddles our desired time.
7. Enter TABLE 3 – *Height Of Tide At Anytime*

Wilhelm's School Of Navigation

    a. On left is *"DURATION"* of rise or fall. Enter to the nearest duration value computed - select closest value. Look right along horizontal line for *"TIME OF NEAREST TIDE"*,

    b. At top of columns shows *Time from nearest high water or low water*. The intersection of *"DURATION"* line with the *"TIME OF NEAREST TIDE"* column determines the correct column to follow down to *corrected height*.

    c. Looking down the correct intersected column that intersects with nearest tabular value for *"RANGE"*.

    d. Take out correction that is subtracted from high water or added to low water depending on *"TIME OF NEAREST TIDE"*.

8. This equation eliminates TABLE 3.and provides greater accuracy:
    "DURATION" in decimal X *"RANGE"* = Correction factor

WORK FORM – Time Of Nearest Tide And Range

ITEMS	Time HW	Time LW	Duration	Height HW	Height LW	Range
Nearest Tide						
Desired Time						
Difference						

WORK FORM – Factors Required For Entering TABLE 3.

DURATION TIME OF RISE OR FALL OF TIDE	
TIME FROM NEAREST HIGH OR LOW TIDE	
RANGE OF TIDE	

WORK FORM – Calculate Water Depth At Desired Time

ITEMS	HW	LW
CHARTED DEPTH OF WATER "DATUM"		
ADD/SUBTRACT TIDE HEIGHT TO DATUM		
SUM		
ADD/SUBTRACT CORRECTION FACTOR		
WATER DEPTH AT DESIRED TIME		

Tidal Current Calculation:

Procedure and instruction for speed of current at any time:

9. Enter Table 2 – *Current Differences And Other Constants*

    a. Look up "PLACE" - Harbor of interest where water current is required

    b. Extract (1) time of flood/ebb and (2) maximum speed flood/ebb together with direction plus (3) reference station

    c. Make note of these three enumerates on your worksheet

Wilhelm's School Of Navigation

10. Enter Table 1 – *Daily Current Predictions*
    a. Look up reference station page with date of inquiry.
    b. Note time of slack to flood or slack to ebb that straddles desired time.
    c. Extract the time slack to flood or slack to ebb, plus speed in knots that straddles desired time.
    d. Make note of these enumerates on your worksheet.
    e. Allow for Daylight-saving Time, if applicable.

11. Correct Time and current speed Extracted From TABLE 1
    a. Add / subtract as indicated the time difference taken from Table 2.
    b. Add / subtract or multiply water height differences taken from Table 2.
    c. Correct using algebraic signs – (" * " asterisk denotes multiply)
    d. Enter results (enumerates) on WORK FORM

12. Compute *"DURATION"* by subtracting. That is the difference between the time of high and low water establishes the duration of the rise or fall.

13. Compute *"TIME OF NEAREST TIDE"*, which is the time difference between desired times and closest high or low water. In other words, the least or smallest time from desired time to high or between desired time and low water.

14. Compute *"RANGE"*, which is the difference in feet between the high and low water that straddles our desired time.

15. Enter TABLE 3 – *Height Of Tide At Anytime*
    a. On left is *"DURATION"* of rise or fall. Enter to the nearest duration value computed - select closest value. Look right along horizontal line for *"TIME OF NEAREST TIDE"*,
    b. At top of columns shows *Time from nearest high water or low water*. The intersection of *"DURATION"* line with the *"TIME OF NEAREST TIDE"* column determines the correct column to follow down to *corrected height*.
    c. Looking down the correct intersected column that intersects with nearest tabular value for *"RANGE"*.
    d. Take out correction that is subtracted from high water or added to low water depending on *"TIME OF NEAREST TIDE"*.

16. This equation eliminates TABLE 3.and provides greater accuracy:
    "DURATION" in decimal X *"RANGE"* = Correction factor

Wilhelm's School Of Navigation

AZIMUTH (Any Body):

Charts and publications are important navigational aids. It is desirable that the celestial navigator has knowledge as to what information is available. The basic Celestial Publications include but are not limited to:

1. *Sailing Directions*
2. *Nautical Almanac*
3. Navigational Tale H.O. No. 229
   (Table of Computed Altitude and Azimuth,
4. Plotting Charts
5. Plotting Sheets

Azimuth (Sun) - an azimuth or bearing of the Sun is required for compass adjustment. Azimuth is relative to compass north that is the relation of the Sun's True North angle to the steering compass. There are some inspection tables providing an azimuth angle, however, it is easer to compute the angle with a Texas Instrument *TI-30Xa* calculator. Azimuth can be determined at a time certain by the following equation as shown:

$$\text{Ship's Latitude} = L$$
$$\text{Sun's Declination} = D$$
$$\text{Meridian Angle} = t$$

$$\left[\sin L \times \sin D + \cos L \times \cos D \times \cos t \right] = 2^{nd} \cos (\text{STO } 3)$$

$$\frac{\sin D - \cos t \times \sin L \div \sin t}{\cos L} = \text{True Bearing Celestial Body}$$

Time and altitude azimuth is computed with the meridian angle. In west longitude the *meridian angle* (t) is the difference between *Greenwich Hour Angle (GHA) and ship's longitude*. The t angle can never exceed 180°. If the angle is greater than 180° it is the *Local Hour Angle* (LHA) subtract from 360° to obtain the *meridian angle* (t). In west longitude, subtract ship's longitude from the GHA. In east longitude, add GHA and ship's longitude together and if greater than 360°, subtract 360° from sum.

Greenwich Hour Angle along with *Declination* is found within the daily pages of Nautical Almanac. The object of the Nautical Almanac is to provide the mariner with a convenient form, the data required for the practice of astronomical navigation at sea. Almanac consists of data from which the *Greenwich Hour Angle* (GHA) and the *Declination* (Dec) of all celestial

Wilhelm's School Of Navigation

bodies used for navigation can be obtained for any instant of *Universal Time* (UT), or *Greenwich Mean Time* (GMT). The *Local Hour Angle* (LHA) or *Meridian Angle* (t) can be obtained by means of the formula:

West longitude (GHA - ship's longitude = LHA and t angle
East longitude (GHA + ship's longitude = LHA and t angle

Solution for solving a timed azimuth is computed with *meridian angle* (t), *declination* (dec), and ship's latitude as the known quantities, the most common formula being that shown in above paragraph. The one problem most students of navigation have is determining whether to label the t angle east or west. If LHA is less than 180°, then LHA = t angle and labeled west. If LHA is greater than 180°, then t angle equals 360° minus LHA and labeled east. Or simply label all normal right side up subtractions as west and all up side down subtractions east. Up side down refer to the longitude being a larger number than the GHA. To illustrate, let us consider the following example:

> EXAMPLE: *Sun was observed at 15h 47m 13s UT on August 24, 2001, when the ship was 27° 33.7N, 72° 32.5W. Required the GHA and Dec of the sun.*

	GHA	Dec
Daily page, August 24 - 15h	44° 25.6	N10° 56.3
Increments 47m 13s	11° 48.3	- 00° 00.7
Sum = GHA / Dec	56° 13.9	N10° 55.6
Longitude of ship	72° 32.5 west	
Meridian / LHA angle	16° 18.6 east	

Enter the 2001 *Nautical Almanac* white page dated 24 August, looking down the right hand page in first column under UT you see 15, this represents the time 15 hours. Directly to the right, on the same line as the 15 in the GHA column take out 44° 25.6, and directly to the right of the GHA number take out the DEC, N10° 56.3. Since the longitude is known, you insert the numerates in the above form and solve for the *t angle* and *declination*.

The azimuth is computed using the equation given on page 58. *Latitude, declination, and meridian angle* have been calculated as shown. Latitude and declination are given negative signs if south. To solve using the Texas Instrument TI-30Xa you enter these three factors into memory and keystroke the equation as follows:

TI-30Xa Calculator

KEY	KEY	DISPLAY	FUNCTION

Wilhelm's School Of Navigation

27.3342	2nd DMS STO 1	27.56166667	Ship's latitude
10.5536	2nd DMS STO 2	10.92666667	Declination
16.1836	2nd DMS STO3	16.31	t angle
RCL 1 sin	X	0.462703023	Latitude
RCL 2 sin	+	0.08770649	Declination
RCL 1 cos	X	0.886513346	Latitude
RCL 2 cos	X	0.981870597	Declination
RCL 3 cos	=	0.923118089	"t" angle
2nd cos	STO 3	22.61373166	Store memory 3
RCL 2 sin	-	0.189552447	Declination
RCL 3 cos	X	0.923118089	"t" Angle
RCL 1 sin	= /÷	-0.237577084	Latitude
RCL 3 sin	÷	-0.617859156	"t" Angle
RCL 1 cos	= 2nd cos *	134.1831431	Result = 134°

- Note The answer *"Azimuth"* (Zn) if t angle is east otherwise subtract 360° if t angle is west. Take absolute value.

AMPLITUDE (Any Body):

Amplitudes are used for checking the compass given that a computation for *Greenwich Hour Angle* (GHA) is not required. Amplitudes are observed when the sun or moon or other celestial body is at a low altitude because it can be measured easiest and most accurately. If a celestial body is observed when its center is on the celestial horizon, the amplitude can be taken directly from table 27, American Practical Navigator.

When the celestial body is raising a prefix E (east) is assigned, and if setting W (west) is assigned. It is given a suffix N (north) or S (south) to agree with the *declination* of the celestial body. The celestial horizon is 32 minutes above the visible horizon. When the center of the sun is on the celestial horizon, its *lower limb* is 21 minutes or two-thirds of a diameter above the visible horizon. When the center of the moon is on the celestial horizon, its *upper limb* is on the visible horizon. When planets and stars are on the celestial horizon, they are a little more than one sun diameter above visible horizon.

Wilhelm's School Of Navigation

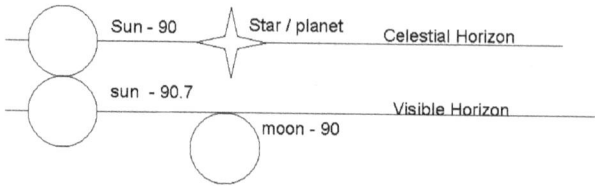

The Bowditch Table 27 is not recommended

The recommended procedure, when a celestial body is on visible or celestial horizon, is to solve for an amplitude using the equation presented on 61. One nice thing about amplitudes, a sextant is not required. The *dead reckoning* latitude and longitude and t angle are known and only the *declination* is necessary. Open the *Nautical Almanac* to a white page holding the correct date, looking down the *Universal Time* column with the time of observation take out *declination* for sun, moon or star under Dec heading. At this point you possess the essential three item, ship's latitude, declination, and t angle necessary for a solution. Mathematical equation is presented within appendix.

To illustrate the aforementioned discussion the following example is presented:

Example: *Cargo ship Brazilian Reefer desires to determine the gyro error on January 22, 1981 in DR position 31°10.0N; 088°00.0W. Gyro bearing of the sun with its center on visible horizon was 247.9°, the Universal Time (UT) was 23h 06m 00s.*

Item	White Keys	Brown / Green Keys
Ship's latitude N +	31.1000	2nd DMS STO 1
Declination S -	19.3112	2nd DMS
South dec. assign negative	(+ ↔ -)	STO 2
"t" angle	90.7	STO 3
Recall RCL	2 sin	-
Recall RCL	3 cos	X
Recall RCL	1 sin	=
Divide		÷
Recall RCL	3 sin	÷
Recall RCL	1 cos	=
Yellow key	2nd	COS
Bearing if east	112.5281	-
Subtract 360° for west	360.0000	=

Wilhelm's School Of Navigation

True Bearing	247.4719	
Subtract gyro bearing	247.9000	
Gyro Error	000.4000	West

Gyro error is labeled west because the 0.4 differences must be added to the True bearing in order to arrive at the correct gyro reading. West is considered plus or add while east is considered a minus to be subtracted.

Prior to storing latitude, declination, and "t" angle convert from minutes and seconds to decimal form. Navigational positions are presented in degrees, minutes, and tenth of minutes. First multiply the tenth of minutes by 60 to arrive at seconds. Enter the degrees, a decimal point followed by minutes and seconds without a space or point. In order to convert this number from degrees, minutes, and seconds, enter 2nd DMS-DD key. Now store into memory with the STO key, which is (STO 1), (STO 2), and (STO 3).

> NOTE: If for some reason your numbers are consistently different, make sure that *DEG* appears above the zero when the calculator is turned on. If RAD or GRAD appears in top right corner depress the DRG key until DEG appears.

COMPASS ERROR AND LEEWAY:

Magnetic compass plus leeway errors create concern for navigators. The reason, ship's steering compass is not equivalent to direction taken from a chart. Directions, relative to the northerly direction along a geographic meridian, are **true**. Ship's *course (track)* should be plotted and logged as true the reference direction and adjusted for *variation, deviations,* and external force of wind or sea. Each compass is equipped with a *lubber line* that is horizontally mounted and oriented with ship's *keel* so that vessel is headed in the direction of intended track.

One of two magnetic compass errors *variation* is the angular difference between true north and magnetic north. This difference caused by terrestrial magnetism, known as *variation* (V) is the same on all points of the compass. Variation error is published on navigational charts inside the magnetic compass rose. Variation is revealed and valid only on the date of chart publication. It is shown in degrees, labeled east or west, along with annual minutes of increase or decrease. It is named east or west to indicate if variation is to be added or subtracted to or from true north. When *uncorrecting* for the variation from true north, algebraic signs (-) or (+) are specified respectively for east and west.

Magnetic Compass (MC) is the result obtained from subtracting or adding variation to or from true north, (uncorrecting). A navigator must first compute the amount of variation to be applied. To obtain this correction multiply the difference in years by the minutes shown, add or subtract this result to variation shown in the Compass Rose. This results in the amount of variation to be added to or subtracted from true *course.*

Wilhelm's School Of Navigation

EXAMPLE: *The cruse ship Ecstasy is underway from Charleston to Liverpool, steering a course of 037°, on July 4, 1990. The annotations inside the compass rose, on a chart dated 1985, shows 6° of west variation with 5' increase at this latitude. What Is the Magnetic Course to steer?*

Year	Degree	Increase
1990	06° 00'	
1985	00° 25'	5' X 5 years
0005	06° 25'	

Variation is 06° 00' west because 25' is less than 30', half a degree.
COMPUTATION FOR MAGNETIC COURSE (MC)

Ship's Course or track	(TC)	037°
Variation	(V)	006° W
Magnetic Course	(MC)	043

Deviation (Dec) is the angular difference between magnetic north (MC) and compass north (CC). It is expressed in degrees and labeled east or west to indicate if this error is to be subtracted (east) or added (west). The deviation error is different on each point of the compass. Iron or electrical fields that influence the magnetic field cause this difference (deviation) of a particular magnetic compass course. Result is a course that indicates something other than the magnetic course (MC). This is the reason for navigators need to eliminate deviation.

EXAMPLE: *The cruse ship Ecstasy is underway from Charleston to Liverpool, steering a course of 037°, on July 4, 1990. The annotations inside the compass rose, on a chart dated 1985, shows 6° of west variation with 5' increase at this latitude. Deviation on this heading is 3° E . What Is the Compass Course to steer?*

SOLUTION FOR UNCORRECTING COMPASS

TC	V	MC	D	CC
037°	6° W	043°	3° E	040°

Leeway is the result of an external force, ensuing from current and or wind, exerting a leeward motion on the vessel. Leeway may be expressed as distance, speed, or angular difference between course steered and track. The external force varies with speed and relative direction of wind, type of vessel, amount of freeboard, trim, and speed of vessel, sea state, and water depth. Most convenient method of applying leeway is adding or subtraction its effect to compass course (CC). Leeway is the result of computing the effects of set and drift and when applied to the compass course (CC) provides the per steering course (psc). The direction in which the water is moving, direction of push, is called *set,* and the speed of the set is called *drift.*

When the relative motion of the set pushes on the starboard side of a vessel the algebraic sign (+) is assigned. Similarly when the relative effect of the set

Wilhelm's School Of Navigation

exerts its force on the port side the algebraic sign (-) is assigned. Therefore we need to determine on which side the dominant force exerts its influence.

> EXAMPLE: *The cruse ship Ecstasy is underway from Charleston to Liverpool, steering a course of 037°, on July 4, 1990. The annotations inside the compass rose, on a chart dated 1985, shows 6° of west variation with 5' increase at this latitude. Deviation on this heading is 3° E . Leeway was computed to be 7° with wind on port side of vessel. What Is the Compass Course to steer?*

SOLUTION FOR UNCORRECTING COMPASS

TC	V	MC	D	CC	L	psc
037°	6° W	043°	3° E	040°	- 7°	033°

COURSE TO STEER (Course in a current):

An external dominant force of wind, sea or a combination thereof affects a course in current. This external force exerts pressure on the bow that retards forward motion or pushes the stern to increase speed. Calculating current affect by subtracting or adding external force speed to vessel's speed is not that simple. A majority of the time the current or force has any of a possible 360° influences on the vessel. The relative bearing of the *leeway* is a necessary consideration for a solution. See page 42 Course to Steer by Leeway equation.

Before proceeding further the student needs to understand nautical terms use in this explanation:

> *Course* - the direction to destination of a vessel used for *dead reckoning*. "C"
> *Speed* - time in hours and minutes it taken to travel one nautical mile. "S"
> *Track* - expected path over bottom (true) considering set and drift. "TR"
> *Speed of advance* – intended rate of travel along intended track. "SOA"
> *Course Over Ground* – actual path traveled "COG" "course made good CMG"
> *Speed Over Ground* - actual rate of travel accomplished
> *Vector* - mathematical term for a line having magnitude and direction.
> *Leeway* - number of degrees needed to off set external force of wind or sea.
> *Set* - direction vessel is being pushed.
> *Drift* - speed vessel is being set.

Leeway by definition is the leeward (away from the wind) motion of a vessel because of external force of wind or sea. By considering the wind and sea forces as one force there is no need to consider them separately. The leeward motion of a vessel is the result of two factors, *set* and *drift*. Drift is the speed that a vessel is set (direction of vessel) by these external forces.

The relative bearing of *leeway* is determined by subtracting ship's heading from the true bearing of the external force, *set*. The acronym, (THER) may be helpful in remembering this equation . T stands for *True Bearing* of the set. H stands for ship's heading or the intended course. E is to remind you of equals, and R stands for *relative bearing* of the set. To illustrate:

Wilhelm's School Of Navigation

EXAMPLE: *The Gulf Stream runs north at and average speed of 2.5 knots. What is the relative bearing of the Gulf stream on a vessel steaming a course of 090°?*

$$\begin{array}{ccc} \text{TB} & \text{SH} & \text{RB} \\ 360° & - 090° & = 270° \end{array}$$

When solving a current problem calculate leeway, which is the result of set and drift. This may be accomplished either of two ways, Texas Instrument calculator TI30Xa, or by a vector diagram. When solving with a vector diagram:

> 1. Draw a vector diagram with course vector the length in units of speed from center of a Maneuvering Board or Compass Rose in degrees of direction intended.
> 2. From center of diagram draw length of set vector, (current vector) in units of speed in degrees in direction of leeward motion.
> 3. Set dividers for vessel's speed, place left point at end of current vector and swing an arc across course vector.
> 4. A line from end of current vector and arc point represents heading necessary to make intended track.
> 5. To read correct heading walk line with parallel ruler, parallel to center of compass rose and where line crosses compass rose read degrees.
> 6. The difference between course line and parallel line is the leeway.

Solving a current problem using a Texas Instrument calculator, TI30Xa, the relative bearing of the set is computed first, and entered into the following equation:

$$\begin{array}{ll} \text{D} & = \text{drift} \\ \text{RBS} & = \text{relative bearing of set} \\ \text{S} & = \text{vessel's speed} \end{array}$$

$$\frac{\text{D X RBS sin}}{\text{S}} = 2^{nd} \text{ SIN Answer is Leeway}$$

$$(\text{Leeway cosin X S}) + (\text{D X RBS cosin}) = \text{SOA}$$

EXAMPLE: *The bulk carrier Global Star plans a voyage from Fort Pierce Florida to Freeport Grand Bahama Island on a true course of 105°, speed 12 knots. Expected set and drift crossing Gulf Stream is north at 3 knots. What is the leeway and SOG?*

$$360° - 105° = 255° \text{ RB}$$

$$\frac{3 \text{ X } 255° \sin}{12} = 14°$$

$$(13.97399363 \cos \text{ X } 12) + (3 \text{ X } 255° \cos) = 10.9\text{k}$$

Wilhelm's School Of Navigation

COMPASS DEVIATION:

A ship's magnetic compass is in an environment rich with electronic fields and steel, which has its own magnetic force influencing the earth's natural magnetism. These peripheral influences cause the compass to deviate from its standard alignment with earth's magnetic field. Deflection of the compass from normal magnetic north orientation is known as *deviation*.

Variation, is the same on all points of the compass representing the difference between magnetic north and geographic north. Unlike variation, *deviation* is different on all points of the compass, and represents the local magnetic compass error. Variation changes with different geographic locations on earth's surface. Contrast this to the *deviation* error that has no relationship to the earth surface but only to surrounding metal containing iron and electrical field caused by electronic equipment.

Swinging ship is the technique used for developing a table of deviation inequities. Running different headings around a compass rose and across a *range* recording the ship's compass bearing each 15° is known as "*Swing Ship*". If the *range* is physical (navigational marks) a sight vane such as a pelorus (dumb compass), or hand-bearing compass is employed to record bearing. An appropriate *range* is one that is listed in the *Light List* providing the *true* direction.

Calculate the *magnetic compass* (MC) bearing by adding *variation* if west, and subtracting if east, to the *true compass* (TC) bearing scheduled in the *Light List*. While on the *range* steam toward the lower *range* mark, compare the *magnetic compass* (MC) bearing with bearing read by *steering compass* (CC). If the *magnetic compass* (MC) is less than the direction read by *steering compass* (CC), label the difference (deviation) west, otherwise the deviation is east. To establish successive deviation error, run consecutive headings every 15° across the *range* comparing the *magnetic compass* (MC) with the *steering compass* (CC).

It will enhance the *Deviation Table* if the steering compass is compensated, e.g. removal of as much error as possible. The maximum *deviation* error ought to be about 6°. When the steering compass has been adjusted, or compensated, to greatest possible extent, a deviation table may be prepared from error established by swinging the ship through a range or by sun's altitude azimuth or amplitude for every 15°. When preparing final deviation table plot a graph of differences with east deviation above a zero horizontal base line, and west deviation below. This will allow the navigator to smooth any values that appear not to be consistent with the others. Left hand side of graph indicates deviation values and the bottom horizontally across records compass headings from 15° to 360°.

EXAMPLE: *The Research Vessel Edwin Link desires to determine its magnetic compass deviation. Using the outbound navigation range at Fort Pierce harbor, Florida, which has a true bearing 062° the following magnetic compass bearings, were observed and compared to the uncorrected bearing. The difference between the magnetic heading*

Wilhelm's School Of Navigation

(MH) and the readings taken with a handheld magnetic compass, compass heading (CH) is the amount of deviation. This deviation is labeled west when the MH is less than the CH, and labeled east when MH is more than the CH.

TABLE OF COMPASS BEARINGS OBSERVED				
UNCORRECTING			COMPASS	CORRECTION
TH	V	MH	CH	DIFFERENCE
062°	005°W	067°	070°	3W
077°	005°W	082°	086°	4W
092°	005°W	097°	102°	5W
107°	005°W	112°	118°	6W
122°	005°W	127°	134°	7W
137°	005°W	142°	148°	6W
152°	005°W	157°	162°	5W
167°	005°W	172°	176°	4W
182°	005°W	187°	190°	3W
197°	005°W	202°	204°	2W
212°	005°W	217°	217°	-0-
227°	005°W	232°	230°	2E
242°	005°W	247°	244°	3E
257°	005°W	262°	258°	4E
272°	005°W	277°	272°	5E
287°	005°W	292°	286°	6E
302°	005°W	307°	300°	7E
317°	005°W	322°	316°	6E
332°	005°W	337°	332°	5E
347°	005°W	352°	348°	4E
002°	005°W	007°	004°	3E
017°	005°W	022°	020°	2E
032°	005°W	037°	037°	-0-
047°	005°W	052°	053°	1W
062°	005°W	067°	070°	3W

Modern compasses have adjustable internal magnet steel bars used for compass compensation. There are two bars installed below the compass 90° to each other; one thwart ship, and the other fore and aft. Two setscrews heads located at the base edge of the compass; one marked E-W, and the other N-S is used for compass compensation. Prior to the *swing ship* routine, adjust on cardinal points eliminating as much error as possible.

Run a series of *Deviation Table* under all conditions in which the compass might be used. Run a table with navigation lights, windshield wipers, and electronic equipment in the on and off position. More than one table may be required. Now before preparing the final *Deviation Table*, plot a simple graph of the values recorded. Lay out a horizontal base line in middle of graph from 000° to 360°. Plot easterly deviation vertically above base line and westerly vertically below the base line. Now draw a smooth curve through all points nearest to a whole degree. Observe the following diagram:

COMPASS HEADINGS

7°																										

Wilhelm's School Of Navigation

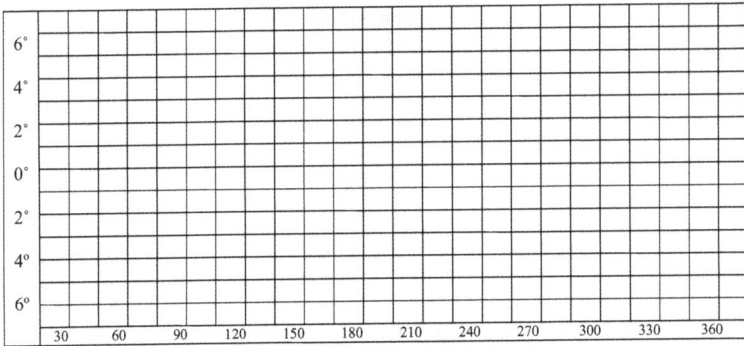

The final *Deviation Table* can be prepared as a direct reading table of critical quantities. The table can be easily used with confidence when verification is prepared each year. Understand that the compass is subject to three magnetic forces, earth's iron core, electrical fields, and metal items manufactured with iron. Deviation varies on all of the vessels headings because of the magnetic material used on board the vessel.

DEVIATION TABLE						
060	074	3W		240	254	3E
075	089	4W		255	269	4E
090	104	5W		270	284	5E
105	119	6W		285	299	6E
120	134	7W		300	314	7E
135	149	6W		315	329	6E
150	164	5W		330	344	5E
165	179	4W		345	359	4E
180	194	3W		360	014	3E
195	209	2W		015	029	2E
210	224	-0-		030	044	-0-
225	239	2E		045	059	2W

ELECTRONIC NAVIGATION:

Electronic navigation is widely used in the air, on land, and sea. Why? Because of inherent accuracy, speed, all weather availability, long range, and ease of uses. Compared to formal navigation skills, an operator can be educated to operate an electronic navigation receiver in a relative short time.

Wilhelm's School Of Navigation

Some of these electronic navigation receiver functions include several different methods, such as, depth sounders, radio direction finder, Radar, Loran C, Global Positioning System (GPS), and Omega.

An electronic depth sounder determines the water depth by measuring the round-trip time for the sounder's transducer to transmit a pulse of ultrasonic energy that travels from the transducer located on ship's bottom to the water bottom, and reflected back to the ship. These electronic pulses generally lie between 50,000 and 200,000 Hertz (cycles per second). This frequency range is beyond the pitch that can be heard by a human ear. Lower the frequency the deeper depths are measured while the higher frequency results in a sharper electronic beam used to measure relative shallow water with better resolution of bottom and fish. Typical receiver takes readings one to thirty per second with an accuracy of approximately ± 5%.

Primary application of an electronic depth sounder is an adjunct to safe navigation. However, sometimes a fix can be accomplished when distinctive bottom topography is available and recorded. When the sounder records a distinctive series of highs and lows that can be found on the chart and compared to the charted bottom features a position is possible. This equipment can provide a great deal of useful information, but care and diligence must be exercised avoiding predictions that may result in loss of situation awareness.

Radio Direction Finders normally receive two frequency bands. The standard "AM" radiobroadcast band you listen to on your automobile radio, and the low frequency beacon band (LF), which is operated by the Coast Guard. Marine radio beacons are located along the U.S. coast. Then again, there are other Radio Direction Finders that receive VHF, and MF signals, generally not used for navigation. The location of the low frequency radio beacons is published in the Light List to assist in identification. Frequencies, schedules of operation, and identifying signals are provided. A 200-mile to as little as 10-mile service range may be expected of this marine beacon. Characteristics of operation of the direction finder's loop antenna in the null position results in a great circle bearing that can be read toward or away and may be affected by *radio deviation* error. Generally it is obvious in which direction the bearing lies.

Radio bearings are taken using these following steps:
1. Align radio receiver with ship's keel, 360° dead ahead
2. Rotate antenna to null point
3. Read *relative bearing*
4. Convert relative bearing to *true bearing* (RB+SH=TB)
5. Plot two or more bearing for a position fix

Wilhelm's School Of Navigation

Radar was originally developed during WWII to identify attacking airplanes or ships, but today it is an exceptional tool for avoiding collision at sea. The visual range of a radar unit depends on height of the antenna. This range depends on distance to the horizon since the electronic pulses do not bend over the horizon. Increased electronic detection of ship traffic, and navigational marks is readily available especially at night or in reduced visibility. Radar presents an excellent navigation tool. Major components of a radar unit is the transmitter/receiver (*Plan Position Indicator –PPI)*, and antenna. Marine radar operates by transmitting brief electronic pulses at extremely high frequency. Theses pulses are reflected or echo back to the antenna, and displayed on the PPI scope, showing range (miles), and relative bearing or true bearing depending on how a peculiar radar unit is configured. All radar bearings are suspect and should not be used for navigation since electronic technicians generally mount antennas without insuring alignment with ship's keel, and the further the range the wider the electronic pulses.

Radar fixes are almost the same as those used for visual plotting, giving due consideration to the unreliability of bearing information. The advantage of radar stems from ability to measure distance accurately. Two ranges off two different navigation marks is the most common radar fix. However, a fix using two ranges off the same navigational mark maybe accomplished by advancing the range on the first navigational mark in the direction of travel, and distance traveled between ranges. At the intersection of these arcs, a fix is established. Or a range combined with a visual bearing for example taken by means of a hand-bearing compass.

Loran-C is an electronic scheme, limited to coastal waters, controlled by an atomic clock using land based radio transmitters. The first is designated as a master station and generally has four slave or secondary stations to form a chain. The master station at a precise time transmits an electronic signal followed by signals from the slave transmitters. The difference in the time of arrival at the ship's loran-C receiver of pulse groups form the master and slave stations is measured by electronic circuitry. The resulting time difference number between the master and slave station determines one line of position, and at the intersection of these numbers form a fix. Electronic ground waves range up to 1,200 miles and are the more reliable when compared to sky waves. Most receivers have a duel display that provides simultaneous readings for two lines of position, thereby permitting an automatic fix. Charts in the coastal and sailing series have the time difference lines (TD) printed in color as an overlay spaced in 5 or 10 units. Using the *Loran Linear Interpolator* published on a corner of the chart is used to solve for the numbers falling between the evenly spaced 5 or 10 unit lines.

GPS (Global Positioning System) is a continuous long-range satellite navigation system for use out of sight of land, and covers the entire world. A GPS receiver acquires time signals from four or more satellites 11,000 miles

Wilhelm's School Of Navigation

high in a 12-hour orbit, and automatically displays vessel's latitude and longitude. Geographic locations (waypoints) are stored within the GPS unit depicting a route of travel, and represent the major GPS advantage of navigating at night or in restricted visibility. Several internal displays indicate ships cross track error along the route of travel. When cruising, conventional navigation techniques require a navigator to compute an ETA, and position update every hour. GPS unit updates the geographic position continuously. The GPS error of 15 meters is enhanced by WAAS system, and other systems which are short range schemes designed for aircraft, and are not available for ocean travel. The GPS obtains its initial accuracy with three positions to the right of the decimal. The first position to the right represents one tenth of a minute or 607.6 feet, second represents hundredth or 60.8 feet, and the third is thousands of a minute or 6.1 feet.

Following are several other uses for a GPS receiver besides navigation fixes:

1. *Swing Ship* for deviation determination is not a recommended procedure. However, when used with a physical range it becomes a prudent course of action. Set a waypoint about five-mile distance in line with a physical range where possible. Make the first pass on the compass course of the range, and note the difference. The difference between magnetic compass and compass course is the deviation. Now swing ship around the compass 360° taking readings every 15° recording the deviation.

2. When tacking to make the windward mark, there is often a tendency to pinch too close to the wind. The GPS can store tacking or turning points as waypoints, and calculate distance and ETA from present position to a given waypoint indicating the true course from one mark to another. In this manner the optimum speed and bearing are displayed without elaborate calculations.

3. Sail boaters can use a GPS to provide the same information as whole set of racing instruments.

The Omega electronic navigation system does not have the accuracy of a GPS, and uses very low-frequency (VLF) radio waves. This frequency signal has considerable range and stability over day and night paths. Signals from a single pair of stations on a single frequency can furnish a hyperbolic line of position, but rough position knowledge is require to within about four miles to identify the set of lines, called a "lane". By using a second frequency reduces position knowledge to 12 miles or 12 miles for each multiple secondary frequency used. Four frequencies would reduce position knowledge to 144 miles. Two or more lines of position are combined in the normal manner to obtain a fix.

Wilhelm's School Of Navigation

CELESTIAL NAVIGATION

Principals of Celestial Navigation:

As with other disciplines, each profession or trade has a vocabulary all its own. In order to converse with fellow members of your profession or trade you must comprehend that vocabulary which is special and meaningful. Learning to navigate with celestial bodies may appear confusing because of the vocabulary; however, the memorization process is not difficult. A few new words and concepts is all that is required. You do not have to be an Einstein. Knowledge of trigonometric equations is not necessary. Simple arithmetic will do nicely.

All navigation, be it coastal piloting or celestial, start with the basic Dead Reckoning maneuver (DR). DR navigation is the process of keeping track of your vessel's position without accounting for wind or sea current. The time, speed, distance equation, when combined with direction by compass will result in a dead reckoned position. Wind or current over a period of time will abrade the course line and distance traveled, thereby placing a dead reckoned position in doubt. Therefore, a method of establishing one or more lines of position (LOP) becomes essential.

A mariner should not confuse a Meridian passage or local apparent noon solution for latitude with the line of position (LOP) solution. The process of ascertaining a solution for an LOP is known as *sight reduction*. The sight reduction method uses the navigational triangle while the local apparent noon (LAN), historically the first method developed is a relative simple calculation. Using the LAN method a navigator can only determine his position at noon each day which may become a problem.

Basic Concept of Celestial Navigation:

There are lighthouses in the sky. That's right, 57 stars are listed in a book called the *Nautical Almanac*. The Nautical Almanac shows the location or geographical position (GP) of 57 stars, sun, moon and 4 planets for every day of the year. The almanac is published yearly by the U.S. Government. A navigator can measure the height of a celestial body with an instrument known as a sextant. With the observed time and height by sextant, a navigator enters the almanac and extracts the geographical position (GP) of the celestial body observed. With this information the navigator consults a volume of books that contain pre-computed answers known as HO 229. The pre-computed latitude, longitude are plotted on a *Universal Plotting Sheet* to obtain an LOP. With two or more LOP's the navigator can established a fixed position.

Wilhelm's School Of Navigation

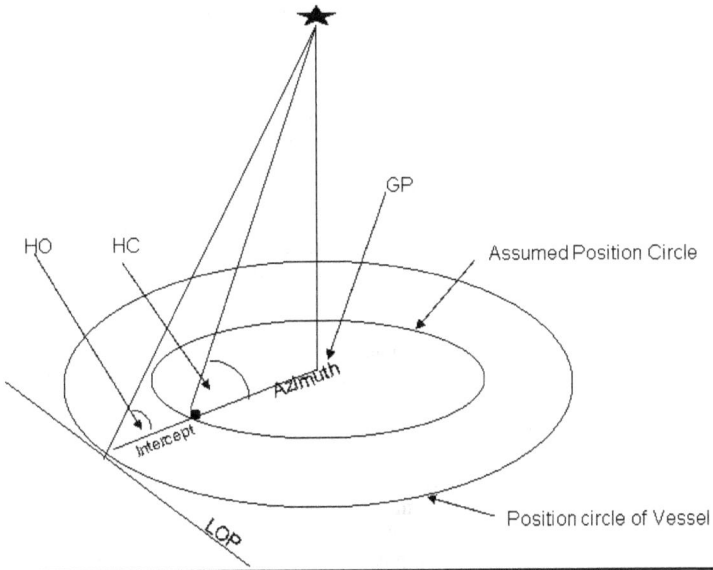

Positions on Earth's Surface:

Navigators have divided the earth into grid lines known as *Latitude* and *Longitude*. The latitude lines circle the earth, measured from the equator (zero°), north (90°) and south (90°) becoming smaller circles as they near the north or south poles. The longitude lines measured 180° east and west from the *Prime Meridian* (Greenwich England) form a *great circle* passing through the North Pole and South Poles. On a Mercator chart, latitude lines are present horizontally, while the longitude lines are shown vertically. This scheme allows any position on the earth's surface to be described by these grid points. An example, Annapolis Maryland, is 38 degrees, 58 minutes north, and 76 degrees, 29 minutes west. By convention, latitude is presented first and longitude second. (38°58'00"N, 076°29'00"W). One degree of latitude or longitude is equal to 60 minutes, and each minute is equal to 60 seconds. Therefore, each degree is equal to 3,600 seconds, (60 minutes X 60 seconds).

Degrees and minutes of latitude are measured from the equator, zero degrees, north and south to 90 degrees, the geographic North or South Poles. Meridians of longitude are measured from Greenwich, England, the Prime Meridian, zero, east and west to the International Date Line, 180°. One minute of latitude is equal to one nautical mile, 6,076 feet or 2,026.7 yards. Only at the equator will one minute of longitude be equal to one nautical mile because the distance between meridians of longitude becomes smaller as they advance toward the north or south geographic poles. For this reason, all

Wilhelm's School Of Navigation

distance measurements on a Mercator chart, use the latitude scale locater on the left and right side of the chart.

The mariner will ascertain in later paragraphs the importance of conversion of meridians of longitude to time. Remember time is longitude and longitude is time: they are both the same quantity, only expressed in a different form. There are two techniques for conversion. One method is to use a pocket calculator that has scientific capacity. With this type of calculator, the navigator reduces the longitude minutes and seconds to decimal and divides by 15 degrees. This result must then be converted back from decimal form to readable time. A second procedure uses the first yellow page in the *American Nautical Almanac*, which is titled, *Conversion of Arc to Time*.

When using the conversion table within the almanac for expression in arc to their equivalent in GMT time, add if longitude is west, subtract if east, to arrive at Greenwich mean time also known as *Universal Time*. There is a difference between *Greenwich Mean Time* and *Universal Time*, however, this difference is small and is discussed under coastal piloting. The table is divided into two sections. The first table shows time under columns of longitude and is entered with longitude at the top. Read down the column: find the whole degree of longitude. Across is the equivalent in time; take out hours and minutes which represent whole degree of longitude. The second table, directly to the right of the first table shows minutes converted to minutes and seconds. Enter second table with minutes of longitude looking down first column. Directly across in the next column, find minutes and seconds of time. Select the next column for minutes that corresponds with minutes taken from first table.

Example: 061°21'W is converted to time by looking in first table, second column for 61°. Looking in next column, hours/minutes we see 4h 04m. We then go to the second table, which is to the right of the first table, looking down the first column for 21 minutes of longitude. Directly across from 21 we select the next column. Take out 1'24" (1 minute, 24 seconds). If the example had been 21 minutes, 22 seconds, the second column would have been selected or 1'25". Since the first column is used, add the two factors together for a' result of 4h05'24" (4h04'00" + 0h01'24").

Conversion using Texas Instrument Calculator, TI-30Xa (61°21'W);

KEY	NUMBER	DISCRIPTION
	61.21	Degrees and minutes
2ⁿᵈ	DMS-DD	Convert to decimal
÷	15	Divide by 15 degrees
=	4.09	
2ⁿᵈ	DD-DMS	Convert to time form
Result	4°05'24"	4h 05m 24s

Wilhelm's School Of Navigation

Local Apparent Time or noon occurs on the standard time meridian when the sun reaches its zenith. This result is known as local mean time within the time zone. Greenwich Mean Time occurs 7½ degrees each side of the zero or standard meridian for a time zone equaling 15 degrees. A standard time meridian occurs every 15 degrees from the zero meridian. Now by adding west longitude and subtracting east longitude, local mean time can be converted into Greenwich Mean Time when the longitude is at a standard meridian, otherwise it is apparent time.

EXAMPLE: *Local time is 08h 20m 15s, and longitude is 010°15.0W. What is Greenwich Mean Time?*

KEY	NUMBER	DISCRIPTION
	10.15	Degrees and minutes
2nd	DMS-DD	Convert to decimal
÷	15	Divide by 15 degrees
=	0.683333333	Equal gives result of division
+		Add
	8.2015	Local mean time
2nd	DMS-DD	Convert to decimal
=	9.020833333	Equal gives result of addition
2nd	DD-DMS	Convert into time form
Result	9°01'15"00	09h 01m 15s Greenwich Time

Celestial Triangle:

On the high seas a navigation position (FIX) is determined by solving what is known as the celestial triangle. This triangle has its three points located at (1) North Pole, (2) the ships position, and (3) the geographic position (GP) of the celestial body. This geographic position is published in the American Nautical Almanac, and represents a position on earth's surface where a line drawn directly from a celestial body to the center of the earth intersects the earth's surface.

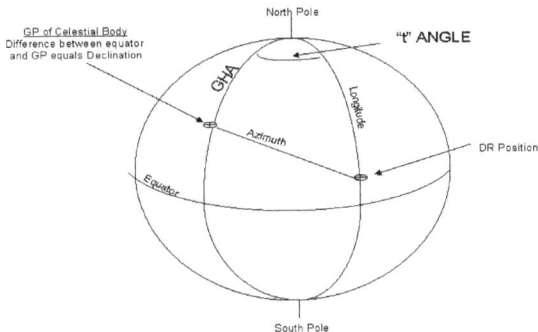

Wilhelm's School Of Navigation

After observing the height of a celestial body, and noting the time, the first step taken in sight reduction, i.e. determining ships position, is finding the geographic position (GP) of the celestial body observed. Accordingly the GP is described by astronomers as *Greenwich Hour Angle* (GHA), and *declination* (Dec.) not by latitude and longitude. The GHA and Dec. for the Sun, Moon, Stars, and plants are found in the pages of the American Nautical Almanac. An oversimplified navigator's definition of declination is simply considered as latitude. Likewise, GHA is though of as longitude. Therefore, to find the GP of a celestial body the navigator simply looks into the American Nautical Almanac extracting the GHA and Dec. at the time of observation.

The difference between a ship's DR longitude and GHA is designated *Local Hour Angle* (LHA) or *"t"* angle. If the difference or angle is 180° or less, it is designated as *"t"* angle otherwise it is the LHA. 360° less the *"t"* angle equals the LHA. To solve a sight reduction problem the (1) DR latitude is required plus (2) Declination, and (3) the LHA or *"t"* angle. With the DR latitude, Declination of celestial body, and the *"t"* the necessary data for a solution is complete.

GP	=	Geographical position of celestial body
GHA	=	Greenwich Hour Angle
DR	=	Dead Reckoning
Dec.	=	Declination of celestial body
LHA	=	Local Hour Angle
t	=	*"t"* angle is180° or less (greater less 360°)

One method for solving the navigational triangle, or sight reduction, is found in six published volumes, known as HO-229. The HO-229 publication provides the answer for each whole number of latitude, Declination, and LHA. Remember all *"t"* angles are less than 180°, the other half is the LHA. These six volumes of HO-229 not only provide answers for whole numbers, but cover the entire earth. To reiterate, on any particular day, at a certain time, a navigator can establish a position by observing the altitude of a celestial body using a sextant, and then consulting HO-229 to obtain the published altitude at an assumed position. By comparing the observed altitude with published altitude, the difference is attained. Knowing this difference a line of position is established.

Time and Celestial Navigation:

Celestial sight reduction depends on accurate time. Correct time is essential. As the earth orbit the Sun, the earth rotates on its axes resulting in local apparent noon occurring at a different time each day because the rotation speed varies. This difference or equation of time is shown on the lower right hand corner of the daily pages of the American Nautical Almanac. In

Wilhelm's School Of Navigation

addition, local apparent noon may be ahead or behind local mean time when the longitude is not on the standard meridian.

The earth being considered a circle 360° divided by 24 hours results in each time zone equaling 15° or one hour. Time zones are measured 12 zones west (+) and 12 zones east (-). The origin for measurement commences at the *Prime Meridian*, Greenwich, England, (zero time zone), east (-) and west (+) to the International Date Line (180° of longitude). Nevertheless, local apparent noon cannot occur at the exact same time on each meridian within the 15° zone. The Prime Meridian, zero, is the standard meridian for the zero time zone which extends 7½° east and west. This is the reason that local mean time or average time is used. Noon occurs within each time zone when the sun reaches its zenith at the standard meridian for that zone. Therefore, all time within a zone is the same as the standard meridian. A standard meridian is placed every 15° east and west from the Prime Meridian, zero to the International Date Line.

Local apparent noon is called LAN or visual sun time. When the sun reaches its zenith on your meridian, you are observing local apparent noon. However, LAN can occur as much as 30 minutes before or after noon that occurred on the standard meridian for the zone. The east coast of the United States, west of the 067.5 longitude to the 082.5 longitude line is labeled *Eastern Standard Time*. The 75th meridian of longitude is the standard meridian for the Eastern Standard Time zone (EST). This is the fifth zone west of the Prime Meridian (000°, 015°, 030°, 045°, 060°, 075°).

In springtime daylight saving time is instituted. Clocks are advanced one hour. In reality, the time zone is moved one zone east. Eastern Standard Time (zone +5 *Romeo*) is replaced with Atlantic Time (zone + 4 *Quebec*). In the fall of the year Quebec zone is replaced with Romeo.

Apparent time is the actual sun time on your meridian. As previously stated the Sun completes one circuit of the earth in one mean (average) solar day and when divided into 24 equal parts results in one hour increments or 15° (360° ÷ 24). The hours are further sub-divided into 60 uniform minutes or 3,600 seconds. The initials h, m, s, are symbols for hours, minutes, seconds. Time aboard ship is maintained on a 24 hour basis; example "10 AM" and "10 PM" are written as 1000 and 2200 hours respectively. Remember apparent time equals observed time, and while standard time equals average (mean) time within a particular time zone. Greenwich or Universal time equals the time within the Zulu time zone located 7½° each side of the Prime Meridian.

Wilhelm's School Of Navigation

ZT	=	Zone Time
ZD	=	Zone description
ZT+ZD	=	GMT (Greenwich Mean Time)
W	=	Watch Time
WE	=	Watch error
GMT-ZD	=	Zone Time (ZT)

Time Problems encountered by navigators; (1) what is the time zone of the ship vessel, (2) what is the watch error, and (3) what is the zone time?

EXAMPLE: *Ship's DR position is 90° west zone description + 6 (90° ÷ 15°). Navigator's watch indicates 13h 59m 44s when the single side band radio WWV, National Bureau of Standards radio time signals is 2000 hours GMT.*

W	13h 59m 44s	
ZD + 6	06h 00m 00s	
GMT by watch	19h 59m 44s	
GMT by radio	20h 00m 00s	
WE	00h 00m 16s	slow - add
W	13h 59m 44s	
Correct Time	14h 00m 00s	

Since most people commonly borrow units of 10 when subtracting, they become confused with the mathematics of time subtraction. When subtracting minutes of time from an hour, it is necessary to transfer one hour to minutes by subtracting one hour and adding 60 to the minutes prior to executing the math. To illustrate: 20h 00m 00s can be expressed as 19h 59m 60s. This makes the problem of subtracting 19h 59m 44s from 2000 hours easy.

Theory of Celestial Navigation:
Understand that the sextant altitude observed (measured) of a celestial body (Sun, Moon, Planets, or stars), receives parallel light rays. These light rays received by our eye through the sextant mirrors are all direct parallel lines measured above the visible horizon, and will be different at separate locations. This occurs because the visible horizon is a plane tangent to the earth's surface at the point of observation. A correction is then required to bring the parallel light ray from earth's surface to earth's center. This correction is known as *altitude correction*, and is extracted from the first page, inside cover, of the Nautical Almanac.

By comparison of the height observed (Ho) by sextant, and the height calculated (Hc) for the assumed position of the celestial body the distance may be computed establishing a line of position (LOP). If the height observed (Ho) was accomplished directly under a celestial body at its GP, the altitude

Wilhelm's School Of Navigation

would be 90°. As we move away from the GP, the angle decreases until it meets the horizon at zero altitude.

A single observation will not provide a fixed position, only a line of position (LOP). However, when the altitude observed is less than 90° (GP), the observer will be located on a circle on the earth's surface having its center at the GP. The radius of this circle equals the observed altitude. We may safely assume that our position will be somewhere on the circle at that moment in time of the observation.

American Nautical Almanac:

American Nautical Almanac is published annually, jointly by the U.S. Naval Observatory and H.M. Stationary Office, London, England. This almanac provides astronomical data required by mariners. Data includes Greenwich Hour Angle and declination for all celestial navigational bodies, together with sunrise, sunset, twilight, moonrise, moonset and meridian passage for sun and moon. Additionally sextant altitude and height of eye corrections are shown on the inside front cover. All of the aforementioned is exhibited for each whole hour of Greenwich Mean Time. In the back of the almanac there are yellow pages displaying correction for minutes and seconds plus declination. These corrections are applied to the even hours of GHA and Dec., respectively. The very first yellow page is a table dedicated to conversion of arc to time. Other material is available and will be discussed later.

To illustrate how the almanac is used, we will solve a problem finding the GHA of the sun on 8 June 2000, at 15h 25m 32s Greenwich Mean Time. First step is to open the 2000 almanac to the daily page containing 8 June date. On the white daily page, we see that 8 June falls on a Thursday. Next, we look down the column to 15 hours and extract the GHA which is 45° 13 minutes, point 2 (45°13.2). The point 2 represents two tenth of a minute or 12 seconds. At the same time look at the bottom of the column for the d correction of 0.2. The v factor is not used for GHA of sun but latter, step #9 below. We now have the GHA for the whole hours, 15, and the d correction factor but an additional 25 minutes 32 seconds must be added to bring the GHA to the total correct time. This is accomplished by turning to the tinted yellow pages, and finding the 25 minute page. These pages are consecutively numbered from zero to 59. Looking down the left side column of the 25 minute page, we see the seconds. On the 25th minute page with the 32 second line showing on the left and reading directly across Sun, Planet column, the correction necessary to add to the whole hours is extracted, 06°23-0. The solution:

GHA	15 hours	45°13.2
GHA	25 minutes 32 seconds	06°23.0
GHA	15h 25m 32s	51°36.2

Following steps determine the GHA and declination adjusted for v/d correction for Sun, Planets, Aries, or Moon:

Wilhelm's School Of Navigation

1. Open almanac to daily white page corresponding to date of interest.
2. Look down first column for whole hour of Greenwich Mean Time.
3. Directly across from whole hour, extract GHA for whole hour of time.
4. At bottom of GHA column extract *v* correction factor if shown and *d* correction factor. (*v* for Moon or Planet, *d* for Sun, Moon, or Planet)
5. Open yellow page for whole minute, first column shows seconds, directly across find columns for Sun/Planets, Aries, and Moon. Extract minutes and seconds of GHA and add to whole hour of GHA found in step #3.
6. At same opening look across at next three columns of *v/d* corrections.
7. Locate on left side *v/d* correction factor found in step 4.
8. Next to the *v* or *d* correction factor is the correction to be applied to GHA or Declination.
9. "*v*" correction is added if positive to GHA otherwise subtract if preceded by a minus sign, and "*d*" correction factor is added to declination if the Dec. is increasing otherwise subtract if declination is decreasing.

Procedure for star GHA:
1. Open almanac to daily white page (left hand page) corresponding to date.
2. First column left hand page, directly across under 'ARIES" extract GHA of Aries for whole hour of GMT.
3. Next look far right on left hand page, column "STAR", extract SHA + Dec.
4. Turn to whole minutes of GMT, yellow pages, across from second column, "ARIES", extract minutes and seconds of GHA.
5. Compute algebraic sum (GHA) whole hour of GMT, step #2 + SHA, step #3 + minutes and seconds of GMT, step #4.

Now we can move forward and determine the Local Hour Angle (LHA). The GHA tells how far around the earth from the Prime Meridian the GP of the sun is located. A DR longitude of 077°03'08"W, tells how far west of the Prime Meridian our estimated position is located. Consequently, the determination of the LHA is clearly the difference between the GHA and the DR longitude. Continuing with our sun problem in the prior paragraph the following presentation completes one corner of the navigational triangle:

GHA	15 hours	45°13.2
GHA	25 minutes 32 seconds	06°23.0
GHA	15h 25m 32s	51°36.2
GHA	15 hours	45°13.2
GHA	25 minutes 32 seconds	03°18.0
GHA	15h 25m 32s	48°31.2
Add	76° greater than 48°	360°00.0
Sum	Total of 48° and 360°	408°31.2
Longitude	Subtract assumed longitude	077°31.2
LHA	Local Hour Angle	331°00.0

Wilhelm's School Of Navigation

Where did the assumed longitude of 77°31.2W come from, you ponder? The original DR longitude was 077°03'08". The difference between 077°03'08", and 076°31.2 results in the need to obtain an LHA in whole degrees because HO-229, the sight reduction tables, are constructed with solutions for whole degrees of LHA. Hence, for convenience, we move the DR longitude to an assumed longitude in order to obtain a whole degree of LHA. Nevertheless, in addition to the need to obtain a whole degree of LHA we are also controlled by a need to keep our plotting confined to the universal plotting sheet. Therefore, the assumed longitude will not exceed nor be less than one-half degree of our DR longitude. To illustrate:

DR Longitude	077°03.1
Subtract one-half degree	000°30.0
Lower limit	076°33.1
Add one degree	001°00.0
Upper limit	077°33.1

The following work form is used to calculate the LHA keeping the assumed position within the boundaries of the universal plotting sheet. Remember, the assumed position must fall within one degree of the DR longitude. That is split one-half degree more or less than the DR longitude:

GHA	15 hours	45°15.2
GHA	25minutes 32 seconds	06°23.0
GHA	15h 25m 32s	51°38.2
Add	76° greater than 51°	360°00.0
Sum	Total of 51° and 360°	411°38.2
DR longitude	077°03.1W	
Subtract half degree	000°30.0	
Lower Limit	076°33.1W	
Add one degree	001°00.0	
Upper Limit	077°33.1W	
Assumed Longitude	Subtract	076°38.2W
LHA	Local Hour Angle	335°00.0 EAST

As exhibited, the not-to-exceed upper limit is 077°33.1W and the lower not to exceed limit is 076°33.1. Thus the navigator selects an assumed longitude number of 076°38.2W that will cause the LHA to be a whole number when subtracted from the GHA. The GHA of 51°38.2 is added to 360°resulting in a sum of 411°38.2. From this total the assumed longitude of 076°38.2 is subtracted, resulting in 335° East because the GHA is less than the assumed longitude. If the navigator subtracts up side down, the LHA is *EAST;* otherwise, it is labeled *WEST*. Remember this rule because the *East or West* label has nothing to do with a steering compass. It simply indicates that a celestial body is either east or west of observer's position.

Wilhelm's School Of Navigation

Declination – Almanac:

As with the LHA computation, the almanac provides not only the GHA for a celestial body but also its *declination*. Remember the definition for Dec.; latitude and Dec. are similar while latitude shown degrees above or below the equator, the Dec. shows the degrees above or below the celestial equator. When the navigator consults the almanac for GHA, the *declination* (Dec.) is extracted at the same opening of the daily almanac page. The *declination* is found by reading directly across from the GHA for whole hour in the column under Dec noting the north or south sign. To provide the proper algebraic sign to the correction factor, the navigator looks up and down the *declination* column to observe if the value is increasing (+) or decreasing (-). At the bottom of the daily white page, the correction factor for Dec. "*d*" is noted. In the tinted yellow pages, when looking for the minutes and seconds correction, the *declination* amendment is extracted and applied by adding or subtracting to modify the *declination*. To illustrate the *declination* computation the following is presented:

Zone Time	ZT	10h25m 32s	
Zone Description	ZD +	05h00m00s	
GMT	GMT	15h25m32s	

NAUTICAL ALMANAC		GHA	Dec.
White Daily Page	15h	45°15.2	N22°50.7
Yellow Page	25m/32s	06°23.0	
Yellow Page	D=+0.2		+ 00°00.1
GHA / Dec.		51°38.2	N22°50.8

Sunrise Sunset Interpolation – Almanac:

The American Nautical Almanac presents the time of sunrise in increments of degrees of latitude. A majority of the times exhibited on the right hand side of the daily pages are shown in units of 10 degrees. For instance, the navigator needs the time of sunrise on 15 February 1993, at DR position 27°28.2N, 080°17.5W. Step one, consult the almanac extracting the times for 20° and 30°. Since our DR latitude falls between the indices, the navigator needs to adjust for the 7°28.2 difference (20° - 27°28.2N). Step two, calculate the time difference factor. Step three, multiply time factor by the difference factor in decimal form. Step four, apply interpolation factor to the latitude time. This method of interpolation is illustrated:

ITEM	DEGREES	TIME
North Latitude	30°	0639
North Latitude	20°	0629
Difference	10°	0010
Divide difference by 10° (10° ÷ 10° = 0001)		
Time Difference Factor	1 minute	

Wilhelm's School Of Navigation

DR Latitude		27°28.2N		
Whole Latitude		20°00.0		
Interpolation element		07°28.2 or 7.47		
Interpolation Factor (1 X 7.47 = 7.47)				7 minutes

Interpolation Factor is applied:				
North Latitude		20°		0629
Interpolation Factor (7 minutes subtracted)			-	0007
Local Mean Time		LMT		0636
Zone Time	(080°17.5W ÷ 15°)	ZD	+	0521
Greenwich Mean Time		GMT		1157
Zone Description		ZD	-	0500
Zone Time Sunrise on 15 Feb 93		LMT		0657

The almanac delivers the time of sunrise for each ten degrees of latitude which is adjusted to the time at the DR latitude. Difference in time is divided by the difference in degrees, resulting in time correction per one degree which is then multiplied by the difference in decimal latitude. The result is the interpolation factor to be applied to latitude time arriving at apparent time of sunrise.

Steps necessary to accomplish sunrise or sunset interpolation:
1. Open almanac to white daily page with corresponding date.
2. On extreme right hand page find proper table for sunrise, sunset, etc.
3. Extract closest degree greater than DR latitude with corresponding time.
4. Extract closest degree less than DR latitude with corresponding time.
5. Calculate time & latitude differences, subtract greater from lesser.
6. Divide difference in time by difference in degrees resulting time in degrees.
7. Minutes of time multiplied by decimal latitude difference, = interpolation
8. Add interpolation factor to lesser time extracted from almanac
9. Calculate GMT, correct for zone description resulting in zone time

Moonset or Moonrise interpolation – Almanac:
The interpolation for moonset is similar to the interpolation for sunrise. Two days of indices are obtained when solving for moonset, as opposed to one day of indices for sunrise. Working with two days instead of one and an equation are the main differences between these two interpolations. Local Mean Time for moonrise and moonset is interpolated by latitude on the day desired and the preceding day in East longitude or following day in WEST longitude. The difference between the two conclusions is multiplied by longitude divided by 360°. This result is added to the datum for day desired. The final result falls between the two previous computations. To illustrate this procedure, let us consider computing moonset for 12 February 1993 at DR position 27°28.2N, 080°17.5W:

Wilhelm's School Of Navigation

MOONSET CALCULATION

ALMANAC	FEBRUARY 12	FEBRUARY 13
20°	1008	1054
30°	-1024	-1113
10°	0016	0019
Divide 0016 in decimal by 10° = (0.16 ÷ 10°)	0001.36	0001.54
DR Latitude	27°28.2N	
Whole degree of Latitude	20°00.0	
Difference	07°28.2	
Convert to decimal form	7.47 X 1.36 = 12m	7.47 X 1.54 = 14.12

	20°	30°
20° Base Latitude	1008	1054
Time correction (7.47 X 1.36 = 12m)	+ 0012	+0014
Sum	1020	1108
Corrected 30° (13 Feb 93)	-1108	
Difference	0048	

EQUATION:

(Minutes X Longitude) ÷ 360° =	Correction
(0048 X 080°17.5) ÷ 360° =	11minutes

COMPUTION MOONSET:

20° Base Latitude		1008
Time Correction		+0012
SUM		1020
From Equation correction		+0011
Local Mean Time	LMT	1031
Longitude (80°17.5 ÷ 15°)		+0521
Greenwich Mean Time	GMT	1552
ZD (80°17.5 ÷ 15°)		-0500
Zone Time of Moonset	ZT	1052

12 February 1993

Meridian Passage Sun – Almanac:

The lower right hand corner of the daily white page of the American Nautical Almanac discloses the time that the sun will pass the half-way point within a time zone, known as the standard meridian. Refer to Compendium section, *"Time and Celestial Navigation"* for a discussion about the 15 degree time zone. The average time or mean time is computed from the standard meridian located 7½° each side of the standard meridian or every 15° from the prime meridian measured east and west. Accordingly, the navigator must interpolate for longitude and time zone description. Understand that time within a zone is the same throughout while actual or apparent time is different on each meridian of longitude. This requires that longitude or arc be converted to time. This conversion is accomplished by dividing longitude by 15° or one time zone. The result equals the number of hours east or west of the prime meridian.

The following problem delineates the procedure used to solve for *"Local Apparent Noon"*. Determine Local Apparent or meridian passage of the sun

Wilhelm's School Of Navigation

on 12 February 1993, at DR position 27°28.2N, 080°17.5W. As the navigator you look in the almanac on the daily white page dated Sunday 12 February, and find the succeeding:

Meridian Passage	Sun 12 Feb 1993	1214
Equation of time	080°17.5W ÷ 15°	0521W
GMT for LAN		1735
Zone Description	080°17.5W ÷ 15°	0500
Zone time for LAN		1235

Meridian Passage – Moon Upper Limb Almanac:

Meridian passage for moon's upper limb is handled in the same way that meridian passage for the sun is computed. The daily yellow pages of the almanac disclose *"Table for Interpolating Sunrise, Moonrise, etc."* The time of meridian passage must be adjusted for the navigator's DR longitude and zone time description.

To illuminate this procedure, we will consider the following problem. The date, 6 May 1993, at DR position 27°28.2N, 080°17.5W, we desire to ascertain the meridian passage of the moon's upper limb. From the white daily page of the American Nautical Almanac, we look at the bottom of the page containing 6 May, and extract time of meridian passage upper limb column, designated MOON.

Meridian Passage	5 May 1993	2345
Equation of time	Arc to time 080°17.5 ÷ 15°	0521W
Greenwich Mean Time	GMT	2906
Zone description	ZD	0500W
Zone Time for	Meridian passage - 6 May	0006

Nautical Twilight A.M. – Almanac:

The nautical almanac displays two types of twilight, civil and nautical, A.M. and P.M. Most navigators prefer nautical twilight in the A.M. and civil twilight in the P.M. The period of incomplete darkness following sunset and preceding sunrise is rated as how visible the horizon can be observed. Civil twilight has a clear horizon and bright stars. Twilight computation is conducted in the same manner as sunrise. The navigator extracts the time for latitude in whole degrees that straddles the DR latitude, and then determines the time difference for one degree of latitude. This time difference is multiplied by the odd degrees resulting in the correction to be applied to the whole degree of time. This computation provides Local Mean Time, (LMT). Apply the zone description, (ZD) for the zone time, (ZT) of nautical twilight.

Consider the following problem as an illustration. 6 May 1992, at DR position, 27°28.2N, and 080 ° 17.5W the navigator desires the time of nautical twilight:

Wilhelm's School Of Navigation

30°	30°N	0418
20°	20°N	0338
Subtract	10°	0020
Divide	20m ÷ 10° = 2 minutes	0002

27°28.2N
20°00.0
07°28.2N   7°28'12" X 2 = 15 minutes

Twilight	20°	0338
Difference from above		-0015
Local Mean Time	LMT for 27°28.2N	0323
Equation of time	080°17.5W ÷ 15° =	+0521
GMT		0544
ZD	080°17.5W ÷ 15° =	-0500
ZT	Nautical Twilight	0544

Sextant:

The marine sextant is a hand held instrument that is used to measure the angle between the sea horizon and a celestial body. No, a sextant does not provide the observer with a position on earth. It does grant the navigator an altitude or angle that is used to compute a line of position, (LOP). Due to the sextant's indispensable value for determining position at sea, the care given and skill with which observations are made is a matter of professional pride.

<u>SEXTANT</u>

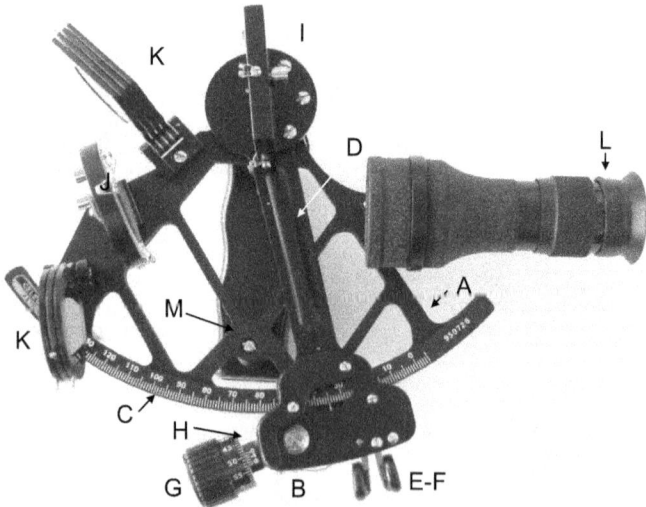

Wilhelm's School Of Navigation

A	=	Frame		B	=	Gear
C	=	Arc		D	=	Arm
E	=	Release		F	=	Trigger
G	=	Drum		H	=	Vernier
I	=	Index Mirror		J	=	Horizon Mirror
K	=	Shades		L	=	Scope
M	=	Handle				

The principle operation of a sextant is to reflect the light rays received from a celestial body by the index mirror to the horizon mirror and then to the eye piece of the observer. The altitude of a celestial body is measured when the index arm of the sextant is rotated to bring the image of a celestial body, reflected into the horizon mirror, tangent to the sea horizon. Sextants are manufactured with two different types of horizon mirrors. One is a split mirror type, where one half of the horizon glass is a mirror and the other half is plain glass revealing the sea horizon. The other type allows the reflection and the sea horizon to appear on one glass.

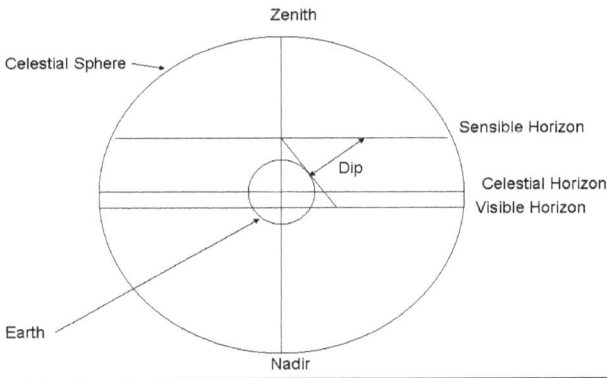

When using the sextant to observe the sun, the sextant is held vertically in the right hand and aimed at a point on the horizon directly below the sun. With suitable glass shades in place, the index arm is moved outward from zero until the reflected image appears in the horizon glass. The micrometer drum, which is mounted on the end of the tangent screw, is adjusted to align the body with the horizon. The sextant is tilted slightly to the right and left to check that the sun is perpendicular to the horizon. Sun will appear to move in an arc. When it is seen at the bottom tangent to the sea horizon and vertical, the arc, drum and Vernier are read. Observations for the moon are made the same as for the sun, using the upper or lower limb. However, stars and planets differ in that the center of a star or planet is brought into coincidence with the horizon.

Wilhelm's School Of Navigation

Reading the sextant altitude, (Hs), is accomplished in three steps. Degrees are read from the arc, minutes from the micrometer drum, and seconds from the Vernier scale in tenths of minutes. This is similar to reading the time by means of the hour hand, minute hand, and second hand of a watch. When the arrow falls between 29 and 30 on the arc, the navigator reads 29°. Now look at the micrometer drum, and seeing that zero falls somewhere between 41 and 42 minutes. This reading is 29 degrees, 41 minutes. Seconds are shown on the micrometer drum where the lines on the right match up with the minute marks. For example, if the number 5 on the Vernier scale matched with a line on the minute scale located on the drum, a navigator would call this reading 29°41.5.

Corrections are necessary to the height by sextant (Hs), observed. The first correction is Index error (Ie). Index error is found by setting the index arm at zero, and observing the horizon. The horizon should appear as a straight line. If the horizon line appears broken, an adjustment is made by rotating the micrometer drum until the horizon is a straight unbroken line. When the error, shown by the arc, is below zero, the amount of error is added to the observed altitude (Hs). If the error appears above zero, the error is subtracted from the altitude (Hs). The rule: *on is off and off is on*, meaning subtract if on the arc, and add if off the arc below zero.

A second correction is required for height of eye above sea level, called *"Dip"* (He). The Dip is always subtracted from the observed altitude. This correction is extracted from the almanac, inside front cover. Enter the almanac with eye height in feet or meters above the water, looking in left column next to height in feet or meters extract correction. The Dip Table is based on this formula:

$$\text{Correction for dip} = 0.97 \sqrt{\text{height of eye}}$$

The third is made for difference between the earth's surface and center of the earth. This modification is also extracted from inside front cover of the almanac. Be careful to look at the proper column for the month of observation. Enter the almanac, inside front cover, with apparent altitude (Ha), which is the result of Hs plus or minus index error (Ie), minus the Dip (He). Appling the *Altitude Correction Table,* (Alt) to the Ha the result obtained is Height Observed (Ho).

There are other corrections, such as a special moon adjustment which will be covered in the sight reduction for the moon. Following are the basic terms and abbreviations used in sextant corrections:

Wilhelm's School Of Navigation

Hs	=	Sextant Height Observed	Ha = Apparent Altitude
Ie	=	Index Error	Alt. = Altitude Correction
He	=	Dip – Height of eye	Ho = Height Observed

Sextant altitude	Hs	31°17.0	Read from sextant
Index Error	Ie	-0°00.5	On is off
Height of eye	He	-0°07.8	Dip table almanac
Apparent altitude	Ha	31°08.7	Sum
Altitude correction	Alt.	-0°17.6	Table – almanac or moon alt. table
HP column almanac	Hp		From altitude table-moon
Upper Limb	30'	-	Mandatory 30 minute subtraction
Observed altitude	Ho	30°51.1	Corrected altitude

Local Hour Angle and Declination Computation:

The sun's local hour angle was discussed in the paragraph that explained the America Nautical Almanac. Nevertheless, the sun, moon, stars and the planets' LHA will be examined in greater detail, along with the time of observation. The very first detail the navigator must deal with is *"time"*. Remember that the local time of an observation must be converted into the time at the *Prime Meridian*, Greenwich, England. Why? You ask. The Nautical Almanac is issued with all enumerates for calculating the *geographic position* of a celestial body at Greenwich Time, zone Zulu (Z). Recall that time zones are 7½° on each side each side of a standard meridian or every 15° measured from the prime meridian. To illustrate this concept consider the following:

EXAMPLE: *On 8 June 1993, at DR position 26°32'53"N, 077°03'08"W, a navigator desires to compute the LHA and Dec. of the sun at 10h25m32s.*

Greenwich Mean Time Computation:

Time of observation	W	10h 25m 32s
ZD 077°03.1 ÷ 15° =	ZD	05h 00m 00s
Greenwich Time	GMT	15h 25m 32s

Enter Nautical Almanac and Extract:

	TIME	GHA	DEC.
GMT (whole hour)	15 hours of GMT	045°14.6	22°52.9N (+0.2)
GMT (minutes)	25m / 32s	006°23.0	
GHA Sun		051°37.6	

Compute Assumed Longitude:

DR Longitude	077°03.1		
Less 30 minutes	000°30.0		
Lower limit	076°33.1		
Plus one degree	001°00.0		
Upper Limit	077°33.1		
Assumed Longitude		076°37.6 W	
Declination (*d correction*)	From yellow page		00°00.1
LHA and Declination		335°00.0 E	22°53.0N

Wilhelm's School Of Navigation

Moon's local hour angle is computed a little differently than that for the sun. Same procedure is used, although on additional correction is required. This correction factor, named *"V"*, is found on the same daily almanac page as the GHA. Shall we scrutinize the subsequent illustration?

Moon 3 April 1993, at 17h40m06s

Zone Time		17h 40m 06s
Zone Description	108°03.1W ÷ 15°	07h 00m 00s
Greenwich Mean Time		10h 40m 06s

	TIME	GHA	DEC. *d*= (+13.3)
GHA – hours	10h	194°57.9	08°14.5
GHA – minutes	40m / 06s	009°34.1	
Correction "v"	8.8	000°05.9	
GHA		204°37.9	

Assumed Longitude	108°03.1		
Less 30 minutes	000°30.0		
Lower Limit	107°33.1		
Plus one degree	001°00.0		
Upper Limit	108°33.1		
Assumed Longitude		107°37.9	
Declination Correction			00°09.2
LHA and Declination		097°00.0	08°23.7N

Planets such as Venus, Mars or Jupiter have their LHA computed in a similar matter as for sun and the same for moon, with one additional correction. Just like the moon which has a "v" correction, planets have a "v" and "d" correction. In other words, a navigator uses the same procedure as' for sun with two amendments. As with all of the prior subjects discussed, we will illustrate with a problem as follows:

Venus 21 February 1993, 18h 38m 13s			
Zone Time	ZT	18h38m13s	
Zone Description	ZD	04h00m00s	
Greenwich Mean Time	GMT	22h38m13s	
	TIME	GHA	DEC.
GHA hours	22h	110°06.4	09°44.8N
GHA minutes	38/13	009°33.3	
V/d Correction		000°00.8	
GHA		119°40.5	
Assumed longitude	064°46.8W		
Less 30 minutes	000°30.0		
Lower Limit	064°16.8		
Plus one degree	001°00.0		

Wilhelm's School Of Navigation

Upper Limit	065°16.8		
Assumed longitude		064°40.5W	
"d" corr from yellow pages			00°00.6
LHA and Declination		055°00.0	09°45.4N

Stars are somewhat different than sun, moon or planets. A new term, *"Sidereal Hour Angle"* (SHA) is used as a correction factor. There are no "v" or "d" corrections when solving for the LHA of a star. The SHA is found in the daily white pages of the Nautical Almanac on extreme right of the left hand page.

The first step in sight reduction for a star is to obtain the GHA of Aries. The first point of Aries uses the symbol of the ram's horns as its designation and is similar to the Prime Meridian since both are starting points. The first point of Aries is the origin of measurement of the sidereal hour angle. Vernal equinox is an expression applied both to the time and point of occurrence when the sun enters the constellation of Aries. Stated in a difference fashion, it is the intersection of the ecliptic and equinoctial, where the declination of the sun's center changes from south to north. To the GHA of Aries, add the SHA, thereby obtaining the GHA of a star. Definition for SHA is arc of the equinoctial, from the hour circle through the vernal equinox measured westward to the hour circle through a point from 0° through 360°. This definition is not of great concern to a navigator, since you need to know only to add the GHA of Aries to the SHA of the star.

In order that the student comprehends our prior discussion of SHA and Aries, we need to depict this dialogue with an illustration:

Rasalhague 1 September 1993 19h 32m 01s - DR 40°N, 30°W

Time of observation	ZT	19h 32m 01s	
Zone description	ZD	02h 00m 00s	= 30° ÷ 15°
GMT	GMT	21h 32m 01s	

	TIME	GHA	DEC.
GHA 21 hours	21 hours	296°01.9	12°34.1N
GHA minutes	32m / 01s	008°01.6	
Sidereal Hour Angle		096°20.1	
Sum GHA	21h32m01s	040°23.6	
Assumed longitude	030°00.0		
Subtract 30 minutes	000°30.0		
Lower Limit	029°30.0		
Add one degree	001°00.0		
Upper Limit	030°30.0		
Assumed longitude		030°23.6	
From yellow page			00°00.0
LHA and Declination		010°00.0 W	12°34.1N

Wilhelm's School Of Navigation

Zone Time for Local Apparent Noon – LAN:

The mathematics encompassing computation for zone time at local apparent noon is made easy when using the Texas Instrument calculator TI-30Xa. In order to conjecture the zone time *polar rectangular* math is necessary since a navigator needs an updated longitude. This is accomplished by advancing the last fix. To illustrate: ship's position on 6 February 1993, was 26°36.0S, 077°13.0E, zone time 0900 hours, course 258° True, speed 19k. At 1000 zone time, the navigator observes the sun for an LOP. The question now becomes, what is the estimated zone time for LAN?

COMPUTATION OF TIME ADVANCED

Almanac daily page (right hand side)	Mer-Pass	1214
Zone Time last fix 077°13.0 ÷ 15° =	ZT	-1000
Time Over Ground (Time Advanced)	TOG	0214
Almanac daily page Mer-Pass		1214
Zone Time of last fix		-0900
Time of advance		0314

TO ADVANCE POSITION (using TI30Xa)

Enter Time 03.14	2nd (DMS)	26°36.0S Lat.
Multiply	X	+00°12.7
Speed	19	26°48.7S Lat.
Equals	=	+26°36.0S
Result is Distance	61.43333	53°24.7 ÷ 2 =
Secondary function keys	2nd (x-y)	26°42.3 Mid Lat.
Course	258	
Secondary function keys	2nd (P-R)	
Correction for DR Latitude	-12.77270821	
Secondary function Keys	2nd (x-y)	
Divide	÷	077°13.0E Lo.
Mid-Latitude (rounded)	27	-001°07.4
Cosine key	COS	076°05.6E Lo.
Result is 67.4 minutes Lo. correction	67.441557	

Meridian Altitude (LAN) – Latitude by Local Apparent Noon):

The following table discloses terminology related for *Meridian Altitude* that is required knowledge for a solution:

1.	Meridian	A line of longitude
2.	Longitude	A great circle running through north and south poles
3.	Meridian Altitude	When celestial body attains it's highest altitude
4.	Local Apparent Noon (LAN)	Sun attains highest altitude at your meridian
5.	Zenith	Top of right triangle – 90° directly overhead
6.	Standard Meridian	Longitude line used to measure time within time zone
7.	Standard time	Time at the standard meridian used within a time zone
8.	Zulu	An acronym for Greenwich time zone
9.	Prime Meridian	Zero longitude line located at Greenwich, England

10.	Time Zone (ZT)	15° wide longitude band 7½° each side standard meridian
11.	Eastern Standard Time (EST)	The time within 7½° each side of 75° standard meridian
12.	Local apparent time	Relative time associated with your longitude
13.	Mean Time	Average time used through out a time zone
14.	Standard Mean Time	Normal watch time within a time zone
15.	Geological Position (GP)	Line drawn from celestial body to earth's center intersects earth's surface
16.	Latitude	Parallel lines to earth's equator 0° to 90° N or 90° south
17.	Sun's altitude	Angle above horizon measured with a sextant
18.	Zenith Distance (ZED)	Angle between zenith and altitude of sun
19.	Greenwich Hour Angle	GHA is Astronomer's term used for longitude
20.	Declination (Dec.)	Astronomer's term used for latitude
21.	Meridian Passage	The act of a celestial body passing over your meridian
22.	Local Mean Time	Local watch time used through out time zone
23.	Hour Angle	Short term used for Greenwich Hour Angle (GHA)

When the sun increases to its highest altitude for the day, noon, we can determine our longitude. Meridian altitude is a rudimentary method for establishing a navigational fix. The term meridian altitude refers to a celestial body, such as the sun, reaching its highest altitude or elevation on any particular day. Example, an observer standing at Cap Henry, Virginia will see the sunrise in the southeast increase in altitude throughout the morning until noon, its highest point or zenith with a bearing of 180°. When the sun's bearing is due south of observer's position, 180°, it's on observers meridian of longitude. Local apparent noon (LAN) occurs when the sun reaches its zenith, bearing 180°, and occurs only when it's on the observer's meridian.

The earth has 24 time zones, 15° wide. Earth rotates on its axis once every 24 hours, a solar day, and completes a 360° circle. Divide 360° by 24 hours, which results in one hour or one time zone. The first time zone, Zulu, located at Greenwich, England is 15° wide extending 7½° each side of zero meridian. Measuring east and west from the *Prime Meridian,* zero, every 15° is another standard meridian with a zone extending 7½° on each side.

Let's clarify the two types of time (1) *standard mean time*, and (2) *local apparent time*. *Standard Mean Time* which is used every day for convenience is determined when the sun reaches its zenith at the standard time meridian located at the center of a time zone. Time within each time zone is uniform; the same, throughout. *Local Apparent Time* occurs when the sun reaches observers local meridian. An example, the 75°W Eastern Standard Time zone extends between 067½° to 082½° of longitude or 7½° each side of standard meridian. When the sun reaches its zenith, at the 75th meridian, the time is noon EST, and local apparent time is also noon at 75th. Everywhere within the zone the time is noon, however, if you are east of the 75th meridian, local apparent noon (LAN) has already occurred, and if west of the 75th local apparent noon (LAN) has not transpired.

The difference between noon at Greenwich, England, and local noon shows navigator's longitude. As the sun moves' across the sky at about 900 knots, a

Wilhelm's School Of Navigation

line drawn from the sun's center to earth's center inscribes a continuous geographical arc or position on earth's surface. This geographical arc is known as the sun's GP, geographic position, at a moment in time. A navigator uses this information to establish a fix. To illustrate this concept, a navigator sets his clock at 12 noon at Greenwich, England, and sails west. Sometime latter the navigator, using a sextant, observes the sun at its zenith. His clock reads 1800 hours, since the sun is on his meridian, bearing 180°, local apparent time is noon. The result of subtracting 1800 Zulu, watch time from 1200 noon apparent time is 6 hours. Six hours is 25% of a solar day, and 90° is 25% of 360°; therefore the longitude is 90° west. If the clock had read 2400 hours, the difference, 12 hours (2400 – 1200) is half a solar day, and half 360° is 180° which corresponds to the International Date Line located in the Pacific Ocean.

Latitude is determined by the sun's angle between the North Pole and the equator. The prior paragraph established a method for calculating longitude at a moment in time, now a method that discloses the navigator's latitude when the sun is on the meridian is reveled. A navigator standing in the northern hemisphere looking at the sun through a sextant measures the angle of the sun above the horizon. This angle, sun's altitude is subtracted from 90° to obtain the zenith distance (ZED). The difference between observer's zenith, observer's geographical position on the earth's surface is equal to observer's latitude. Of course this situation only exists when the sun is on the equator. When off the equator an adjustment becomes necessary.

To solve a Meridian Altitude sight reduction a watch, sextant, and Nautical Almanac is all that is dictated. Look up the geographical position (GP) of the sun at the time the sun's zenith was observed. The almanac describes the sun's GP in astronomical terms known as GHA and Dec. Extract from the almanac the GHA, declination, and *"d"* correction copying onto the *Meridian Altitude Worksheet*. At the time of local apparent noon, the altitude of the sun as observed at its zenith, subtract 90°, add or subtract declination to compute latitude. The GHA at time of sextant observation is the longitude. With latitude and longitude established, a fix is obtained.

In order to solve a meridian altitude question a navigator needs to estimate the time of occurrence for local apparent noon. Otherwise you have no idea when to commence sextant observations. To estimate the time that LAN occurs at your meridian, adjust for the equation of time, which is computed by dividing DR longitude by 15°. This is easily accomplished with TI30Xa calculator or by looking at the *Conversion of Arc to Time* table found on the first yellow page at back of almanac. An example, the almanac shows meridian passage on daily white page, lower right hand side from about 1144 to 1206. As you see these given times for noon are not very accurate since seconds are omitted. Actual time of observed zenith will dictate actual longitude.

Wilhelm's School Of Navigation

Many students find the conversion of longitude to time somewhat confusing. I agree. Degrees are whole numbers, which is a base ten system like dollars, and minutes and seconds are a base 60 system since 60 minutes equal one hour, a whole number. To make matters more bewildering, second are also expressed in tenth of minutes. All of these different confounding mathematical systems must be reduced to one common base. Otherwise, division, and multiplication cannot be computed. The common base is decimal form for minutes, and seconds. To accomplish the conversion of minutes, and seconds to decimal; minutes, and seconds are divided by 60. Example: 80°30.5W, longitude is converted to decimal by dividing the 30 minutes, 30 seconds by 60, which equals 50.5 or a half hour + half minute. Now the longitude can be capable of dividing by 15° (one time zone) or 80.5050. To convert the 50.5 (decimal minutes) back into time form merely multiply .50.5 by 60 equals 30 minutes, 30 seconds. To obtained the correct time zone, change 80°30.5W to decimal (30.30 ÷ 60 = 50.5), and divide by 15°. The answer, 5.367 is now converted to time form by multiplying .367 by 60 for 22minutes plus 5 hours equals 5 h 22m. It is very important that each student comprehend the decimal conversion because it is used throughout navigation procedures.

An example to demonstrate the aforementioned, daily white page of almanac, lower right hand page under MERIDIAN PASSAGE, extracts time of passage:

Meridian passage	11h 46m 00s
Zone Time (ZT) [80°30.5W]	05h 22m 05s
Estimated Time of LAN	17h 07m 05s

A sextant observation of a celestial body such as the sun measures the angle between the observer's horizon and the celestial body. To acquire observer's latitude, the angle observed is subtracted from 90°, to compute distance between observer zenith, and sun's geographical position (GP). Example: sun is on the equator at time of observation having an altitude of 63°, bearing 180°. The closer an observer approaches the equator the greater the angle. If the observer was directly on the equator the angle would read 90°. Likewise the further an observer is away from the equator the smaller the angle. Now let's return to our example of 63°, subtracted from 90° results in a zenith distance (ZED) of 27°N which would equal our latitude as long as the sun's GP remains on the equator. Why? Because the sun's GP, a line extending from the sun to earth's center penetrates earth surface at the equator, and the ZED represents distance between observer and sun's GP.

Sun's GP is on the equator happen only twice a year, and a method is required to compensate for any other day of the year. Astronomers describe positions of celestial bodies by *Hour Angle* (longitude), and *Declination* (latitude). Because the sun's declination (latitude) is either north or south of the equator

Wilhelm's School Of Navigation

an adjustment is necessary to calculate observer's latitude. The following rules simplify this adjustment:

Lat. and declination, same name   - add
Lat. and declination, opposite name   - subtract
Lat. less than declination, same name   - subtract

To clearly understand the sight reduction process, we will use a *MERIDIAN ALTITUDE WORKSHEET*. On 23 November 1997, a ship in DR Lat. 27°26.5N, Lo. 080°16.2W, observes sun's lower limb by sextant, altitude is 41°59.2 at 12h 07m 34s local time. Bearing is south, height of eye 14 feet, index error 1.0 off the arc. What is ship's latitude and longitude at time of our sextant observation?

MERIDIAN ALTITUDE WORKSHEET

Date – 23 November 1997			**BODY**	
DR Lat. 27°26.5N, Lo. 080°16.2W			Sun Lower limb	
ESTIMATE TIME FOR LOCAL APPARENT NOON:			**TIME**	
1.	Local Mean Time of Local Apparent Noon	LAN	11h46m00s	
2.	Equation of Time 080°16.3W ÷ 15° = 5h 21m 05s	ZD	05h21m05s	
3.	Greenwich Mean Time of Local Apparent Noon	GMT	17h07m05s	
ACTUAL TIME OF SEXTANT OBSERVATION				
	Local Time of LAN Observed	LAN	12h07m34s	
	Zone Description	ZD	05h00m00s	
4.	Time of observation in hours, minutes, and seconds	GMT	17h07m34s	
5.	Extracted from Nautical Almanac:			
	Greenwich Hour Angle from Daily page almanac	17h	078°22.7	
6.	Greenwich Hour Angle from yellow pages almanac	07/34	001°53.5	
7.	Total – whole hours plus minutes and seconds	GHA	080°16.2	
8.	Declination (Almanac daily white page – bottom	*d-0.5*	20°26.8S	
9.	Correction of Declination	Corr.	-00°00.1	
10.	Declination at 22h 58m 52s	Dec.	20°26.7S	
11.	Height by sextant	Hs	41°59.2	
12.	Index error	Ie	- 00°01.0	
13.	Height of eye – Dip 14 feet	He	00°06.6	
14.	Result after correction (Height Apparent)	Ha	41°51.6	
15.	Altitude correction-inside front cover almanac	Alt.	+00°15.2	
16.	Height Observed by sextant	Ho	42°06.8	
17.	Subtract 90° for zenith distance	90°	- 89°60.0	
18.	Zenith distance (same name as DR Lat.)	ZED	47°53.2N	
19.	Declination – from computation above	Dec.	- 20°26.7S	
20.	Latitude at time of LAN	Lat.	27°26.5N	
21	Greenwich Hour Angle = vessel's longitude	Long.	080°16.2W	
RULES GOVERNING DECLINATION:				

Wilhelm's School Of Navigation

1.	Lat. and Dec. same name	- add
2.	Lat. and Dec. opposite name	- subtract
3.	Lat. less than Dec. same name	- subtract

EXPLANATION FOR MERIDIAN ALTITUDE WORKSHEET

1. Open 1997 Nautical Almanac, page 227, 23 November, daily white page, lower right hand side, marked *"sun"*, look in Day column for date of observation 23, at the bottom. On a line directly across from the day 23, see 11h 46m under Mer. Pass. This is the time the sun will cross each of the standard meridians.

2. *Equation of time*, simply stated is that one rotation of the earth, a solar day, does not provide an equal uniform rate of rotation to the apparent or actual day. Because the accumulated difference between these times, called equation of time, is continually changing, the period of daylight is shifting, in addition to its increase or decrease in length due to changing declination. Therefore the DR longitude is divided by 15° resulting longitude expressed in time format, called *zone description* (ZD). The very first yellow page at in the back of Nautical Almanac provides a table for *Conversion of Arc to Time*. If ZD is labeled west add, if labeled east subtract to correct for Greenwich time (ZULU).

3. This is the result of adding or subtracting the ZD (longitude ÷ 15°) to local mean time of local apparent noon (LAN) extracted from the Nautical Almanac. The result is the expected time of apparent noon. You should note that the time extracted from the almanac is not accurate because seconds are not included. This is the time where rounds of sextant observations are taken to find exact time of meridian passage.

4. Record the actual time of observation for Local Apparent Noon (LAN). When the sun reaches its zenith as shown by a series of sextant observations, the time is recorded. This time will be used for a solution.

5. Open 1997 Nautical Almanac page 227, 23 November. See daily white page column labeled "sun" on extreme left, at bottom of page, and extract GHA. The GHA, remember is simply the longitude of the sun on the celestial sphere. Column on left of sun, labeled UT shows 17 hours of Zulu time. This is the time in hours of your sextant observation (line 4); now extract 78°22.7 for line number 5. At the same moment it is good practice to extract the declination located directly across from 17 hours, 78°22.7 and S20°26.8. Please observe the *"d"* factor at bottom of page of *0.5*. Note if declination is increasing or decreasing. Enter declination on line 8 along with the *"d"* factor marked with a "+" if increasing, or "-"if decreasing.

6. Open the 1997 Nautical Almanac to yellow page at back of almanac labeled *7m*, for 7 minutes, looking down left hand column under 7, find 34 seconds. Directly across and adjacent to 34 under column labeled SUN PLANTS see 1°53.5. This quantity is added to 78°22.7, line 5. At this instant look across sun, Aries and moon columns to the 3rd column labeled corr. Using the *"d"* factor *"-0.5"* we find our correction as *"-0.1"* on line 9.

7. Add together the GHA of 78°22.7 and GHA minutes/seconds 01°53.5 for total GHA amounting to 080°16.2.

Wilhelm's School Of Navigation

8. Declination was extracted, and entered in line 8, when whole hour of GHA was entered on line 5.

9. Correction to declination is the *"d"* factor found at bottom of daily white page. This correction was extracted at the same moment GHA and declination was extracted. The *"d"* factor is added when declination is increasing, and subtracted when decreasing. On line 6 we were extracting the correction from the yellow pages which was entered on line 9.

10. Corrected Declination plus or minus correction.

11. Read height by sextant from sextant's arc, micrometer drum, Vernier scale. The sextant is held in the right hand and index arm is moved with left hand. Holding the sextant looking at the horizon move the index arm until celestial body appears, turn micrometer drum until body is brought down to the horizon. Rock sextant side to side making sure the body touches the horizon with instrument perpendicular to horizon. Note exact time of observation to the second, and enter time on line 4. Enter height by sextant (Hs) line 11 from the arc.

12. Index error is the result of the index mirror being out of alignment due to use. With index arm set on zero, sight on horizon, if horizon shows an unbroken line, no error exists. A broken horizon indicates an error which is brought to alignment, and index error is read from Vernier scale. On is off (subtract), and off is on (add).

13. Correction for height of observer's eye above sea level is labeled He or Dip. The sun's adjustment is found on inside front cover *A2 Altitude Correction Table 10° - 90°, Sun, Stars, Planets.* Enter table "DIP" with height of eye. Be careful, height is in feet and meters. Be sure you are in legitimate column. Dip is always subtracted, and may be found mathematically [0.97√ height of eye   ]

14. The result of the above computation which may be the sum or difference depending on the amount of adjustments for index error, and height of eye.

15. Altitude correction is extracted from altitude table, inside front cover. Go to inside front cover of Nautical Almanac, see table A2 ALTITUDE CORRECTION TABLE 10° - 90° Sun, Stars, Planets, select column corresponding with month of observation, select column corresponding with month of observation, select correction that falls into range of height by sextant (Hs) reading.

16. Height observed, this is the sum of height apparent (Ha), and altitude correction.

17. Subtract from 90° to obtain zenith angle (ZED). In order to make the mathematics easy, write 90° as follows 89°60.0 or 89°59.10, by performing the borrowing first the chance of error is reduced.

18. This is the zenith distance or ZED. The result obtained by subtracting line 16 from line 17.

19. Now directly copy the amount shown on line 10 on to line 19. In this case subtract line 19 from line 18 to obtain the result or difference which is the Latitude.

Wilhelm's School Of Navigation

20. This amount represents the observed latitude. Line 19 is subtracted or added to line 18 depending on the RULES CONTROLLING DECLINATION.

21. When you copy the amount shown on line 7 into line 21 the result is longitude of observer at time of observation.

RULES CONTROLLING DECLINATION:
1. Latitude and Declination, same name   - add
2. Latitude and Declination, opposite name   - subtract
3. Latitude less than Declination, same name - subtract

Meridian Angle and Local Hour Angle:

As presented in our prior explanation of LHA, the difference between the GHA and vessel's longitude in the western hemisphere is the angular distance westward through 360 degrees. When a navigator desires to solve the *navigational triangle* by an equation using a pocket calculator, the meridian angle or *"t"* angle is used.

The *"t"* angle is computed in the manner as the LHA. When subtracting west longitude from the GHA, and the result is greater than 180°, subtract 360° to solve for *"t"* angle, and angle is *east,* however, if less than 180°, angle is *west.* Also, in eastern hemisphere GHA and longitude are added to solve for *"t"* angle, and if result is greater than 180°, subtract 360°. The *"t"* angle can never exceed 180°. When the angle is exactly 180°, the *"t"* may be either east or west. If the mariner remembers the following rule life is simpler: Subtracting up side down, then angle is labeled east, otherwise it is west. A navigator at sea has an advantage over classroom student, because he can see whether the celestial body is east or west of his meridian. When the LHA is less than 180°, then LHA and *"t"* angle are the same, and angle is *west.*

There is no need to adjust the *"t"* angle to a whole number. The pocket calculator handles the minutes, and seconds easily by turning them into decimal form. This means that an assumed longitude is not necessary, and the navigator may use the DR latitude and longitude. The following arrangement amplifies this procedure.

GHA	059°46.8
DR Longitude	080°17.5
Meridian Angle "t"	020°30.7 E

To reiterate, the meridian angle known as the *"t"* angle is the angular distance that a celestial body is east or west of local meridian, measured the shortest way from 0° to 180°. The *"t"* angle is named east if east of observed meridian, and west if west of observed meridian.

Wilhelm's School Of Navigation

Amplitude:

The navigational triangle is solved by knowing the GHA, declination, latitude and longitude and the LHA or "t" angle. Plus knowing if the body is rising and therefore east of observed meridian, otherwise the body is setting and therefore west of the meridian. Using the six "known items", the navigator may proceed by a choice of methods to find the computed altitude and azimuth of the body.

All navigators need to know their gyro error, or magnetic compass deviation. When the azimuth of the sun is determined and compared to a compass heading the amount of error has been found. When solving the navigation triangle, mariners have two choices, either HO-229 tables or mathematical equation. The equation method is best since copy errors are omitted using less effort. When the sun is on the celestial horizon, which is 32 minutes above visual horizon, use 90° as the "t" angle. If the one half of sun is below visual horizon, use 90.7° as "t" angle. The 90.7° is in decimal form, no need to divide by 60. Also, when moon's upper limb is on horizon, 90° may be used as the "t" angle.

AMPLITUDE WORKSHEET

GMT	00h 00m 00s	Dec.	S00°00.0
Watch Error	00m 00s	"d" Corr.	00°00.0
Corr. Time			
24 hr clock			
GMT	00h 00m 00s	Declination	00°00.0S
Latitude	00°00.0N	2nd DMS-DD	STO 1
Declination	00°00.0S	2nd DMS-DD	STO 2
"t" Angle	90.0	2nd DMS-DD	STO 3
Recall key 2 & sine	RCL	2	SIN
Subtract	-		
Recall key 3 & cosine	RCL	3	COS
Multiply	X		
Recall key 1	RCL	1	SIN
Equals	=		
Divide	÷		
Recall key 3	RCL	3	SIN
Divide	÷		
Recall key 1	RCL	1	COS
Equals	=		
Cosine	2nd	COS	
Subtract	-		
Sun west, minus 360°	360.		
Azimuth			

With a south latitude and/or east longitude, enter a minus prior to the store command. This is how the calculator is programmed to distinguish between

Wilhelm's School Of Navigation

north and south latitudes. Therefore, a navigator enters a minus sign after entering a south latitude or east longitude prior to the store command. Following is the mathematical equations for solving a navigation triangle for HC, height calculated, and Zn, azimuth followed by keystrokes when using a TI30Xa calculator.

$$90° - (\text{Sin Lat.} \times \sin \text{Dec.} + \cos \text{Lat.} \times \cos \text{Dec.} \times \cos "t" = \text{Inv}) = \frac{HC}{\text{Sin}}$$

$$\sin \text{Dec.} - (\cos "t" \times \sin \text{Lat.}) \div \sin "t" \div \cos \text{Lat.} = Z \ (\text{if } "t" \text{ is west -360°}) = Zn$$

Key Strokes TI30Xa Calculator

Latitude	00°00.0N	2nd DMS-DD	STO 1
Declination	00°00.0S	2nd DMS-DD	STO 2
"t" Angle	90.0	2nd DMS-DD	STO 3
Recall key 1 & sine	RCL	1	SIN
Multiply	X		
Recall key 2 & sin	RCL	2	SIN
Add	+		
Recall key 1 & cos	RCL	1	COS
Multiply	X		
Recall key 2 & cos	RCL	2	COS
Multiply	X		
Recall key 3 & cos	RCL	3	COS
Equal	=		
Inverse cos	2nd		COS
Store memory 3	STO	3	
Subtract	-		
Enter 90 degrees	90		
Equal	=		
Height calculated	ANSWER	2nd DD-DMS	HC
Recall key 2 & sine	RCL	2	SIN
Subtract	-		
Recall key 3 & cosine	RCL	3	COS
Multiply	X		
Recall key 1	RCL	1	SIN
Equals	=		
Divide	÷		
Recall key 3	RCL	3	SIN
Divide	÷		
Recall key 1	RCL	1	COS
Equals	=		
Cosine	2nd	COS	Azimuth	if "t" East
Subtract	-		
Sun west, minus 360°	360.		
Azimuth	ANSWER		Azimuth	If "t" West

Wilhelm's School Of Navigation

Intercept Azimuth By HO-229:

The HO-229 Tables contain pre-computed solutions for a whole degree of latitude, and every 30 minutes of longitude. Enter the HO-229 table appropriate for latitude with the LHA, whole degree of declination, and latitude. Extract (1) HC, (2) "d" correction factor, and (3) azimuth "Z" and the "Z" directly below tabulated azimuth. The extracted Hc must be corrected for minutes, and tenths of minutes of declination since a whole degree of declination was used for entry. The first interpolation or correction is minutes of declination multiplied by the "d" factor, divided by 60 found in the HO-229 table. The "d" correction has an algebra sign. No sign indicates a (+) positive number and a minus (-) indicates a negative number. A *dot* (·) to the right of the "*d*" value requires an additional correction (DSD).

This means that a *Double-Second Difference* (DSD) interpolation is obligatory. After calculating the first interpolation, find the difference by subtracting top "d" factor from the "d" factor directly below the tabulated "d". With this difference *Double-Second Difference* and correction table located on front and back cover of HO-229. Extract correction and apply to the tabulated Hc (height by sextant).

The difference between the (1) first tabulated azimuth "Z", and (2) the "Z" directly below is multiplied by the minutes of declination, divided by 60. If the "Z" is increasing this computed result is added to the first tabulated azimuth or subtracted if "Z" is decreasing from the first tabulated azimuth.

Altitude Azimuth:

Mathematical equations required for a solution to an altitude azimuth problem have been provided and discussed in paragraphs on amplitude. These same equations presented are used for altitude, azimuth solution. Both equations are required since the result obtained in the first solution is needed to solve the second equation. So let us examine a problem that will indelibly inscribe this solution into your cranium.

$$90° - \left\{ \text{Inv cos (sin Lat. X sin Dec. + cos Lat. X cos Dec. X cos "t")} \right\} = HC$$

$$\text{Sin Dec.} \underline{- \cos \text{"t" X sin Lat.}} \div \cos \text{Lat.} = ZN \text{ (if west minus 360°)}$$
$$\text{Sin "t"}$$

Illustrative Problem: *21 February 1997, a navigator observes the planet Mars at 0800 zone time, DR position 29°15.0S, 044°12.0E for an LOP. Required the altitude and azimuth of Mars.*

Wilhelm's School Of Navigation

ALTITUDE AZIMUTH WORKSHEET

TIME CALCULATION:			
ZT		0800	Zone time
ZD	044°12.0E ÷ 15°	0300 E	Zone description
GMT		0500	Greenwich mean time

Mars 21 February 2003		GHA	Dec.
GHA hours	5 hours	323°49.8	S23°07.3 (+0.1)
GHA min./sec.	00/00	000°00.0	
"v" corr. Mars (0.7)		000°00.0	00°00.0
DR longitude	044°12.0E		
Less 30 minutes	000°30.0		
Lower limit	043°42.0E		
Plus 1°	001°00.0		
Upper limit	044°42.0E		
Assumed longitude		043°49.8E	23°07.3S
LHA		280°00.0	
Less 360°		360°	
"t" angle		080°W	

STORE IN CALCULATOR:			
Latitude	-29.15.0	2nd DMS-DD	STO 1
Declination	-23.0718	2nd DMS-DD	STO 2
"t" angle	080	2nd DMS-DD	STO 3

KEY STROKES TI30Xa CALCULATOR:			
Recall memory 1	RCL	1 – SIN	-0.488621241
Multiply	X		-0.488621241
Recall memory 2	RCL	2 – SIN	-0.392684923
Add	+		0.191874195
Recall memory 1	RCL	1 - COS	0.872496007
Multiply	X		0.872496007
Recall memory 2	RCL	2 - COS	0.919673067
Multiply	X		0.802411079
Recall memory 3	RCL	3 - COS	-0.173648178
Equals	=		0.331211416
Inverse Cosin	2nd	COS	70.65767997
Store memory 3	STO	3	70.65767997
Subtract 90°	-	90.	90
Equals	=		-19.34232003
Height by sextant	Answer first equation	2nd DD-DMS	19°20'32"
Recall memory 2	RCL	2 – SIN	-0.392684923
Subtract	-		-0.392684923
Recall memory 3	RCL	3 – COS	0.331211416
Multiply	X		0.331211416
Recall memory 1	RCL	1 – SIN	-0.488621241
Equal & divide	=	÷	0.23084799
Recall memory 1	RCL	1 – COS	0.872496007
Divide	÷		-0.264583434
Recall memory 3	RCL	3 – SIN	0.943556568
Equals	=		-0.280410781
Minus 360° if west	-	360°	360
Equals ZN of 360°	=		-360.2804108

Wilhelm's School Of Navigation

Intercept Azimuth:

In most real life situations a vessel's DR plot does not coincide with the time of a celestial observation. A new DR position may be advanced to the time of observation, by a graphical plot of distance run, and course steered. This course advancement can be a cumbersome task on small ships but the TI30Xa calculator makes life easy. Polar Rectangular mathematics provided by the calculator accomplishes this task with ease. Calculation of new DR position by *Polar Rectangular* is accomplished along with the calculation to advance the DR position due to the need for *mid-latitude*.

Illustrative Problem: *11 January 1981, course 223°T, speed 14k, 0500 ZT fix 20°18.0S, 037°56.0W, sun lower limb is observed, Hs 45°23.0, Ie 1.5 on the arc, He 50 feet 0830 ZT, chronometer reads 11h 14m 44s, slow by 15m 03s.*

INTERCEPT AZIMUTH WORKSHEET

TIME OF FIX		TME OF DR POSITION	
Chronometer Time	11h 14m 44s	ZT	0500
Chronometer error +	00h 15m 03s	ZD 37°56.0 ÷ 15° =	0300
Chronometer Time	11h 29m 47s	GMT	0800
Less GMT	08h 00m 00s		
Time of advance	03h 29m 47s		

NEW DR POSITION BY POLAR RECTANGULAR TI30Xa CALCULATOR			
Time of advance	3.2947	2nd DMS-DD	3.496388889
Multiply by speed	X	14	14
Equal distanced run	=	48.9	48.94944444
Polar Rectangular key	2nd	x-y	14.
Enter course 223°	223		223
Difference in latitude	2nd	P-R	-35.79935739 or 35.8'
Polar Rectangular key	2nd	x-y	-33.38344084
Divide by mid-lat *	÷	21 COS	0.933580426
Diff in Longitude	=		35.75850552 or 35.7'

MID-LATITUDE COMPUTATION AND DR LATITUDE LONGITUDE POSITION			
Original DR latitude	Lat.	20°18.0S	
Difference in latitude	dLat. +	00°35.8	
New DR latitude	DR latitude	20°53.8S	
Add original latitude	+	20°18.0	
Sum & divide by 2		41°11.8 ÷ 2	
Mid-latitude	=	20°35.9 or 21°	Enter calculation *
Original longitude	Longitude	037°56.0W	
Diff. in longitude	d Lo. +	000°35.7	
New longitude	DR Longitude	038°37.7	

Updated DR position 20°53.8S, 038°37.7W

Wilhelm's School Of Navigation

SIGHT REDUCTION WORKSHEET
USING ASSUMED POSITION

DATE		BODY	
DR Latitude		Upper Limb	
DR Longitude		Lower Limb	
Sextant Height - HS		Time of Observation	
Index Error – Ie		Zone description	
Dip - He		Greenwich Time	
Result - Ha		Day less 24 hours	
Altitude Corr. - Alt		GMT on	
Moon HP			
Observed height – Ho			
GHA hours		Declination	
GHA m/s		Correction "d"	
GHA sum		Corrected declination	
DR Longitude			
"v" Correction			
Less 30 minutes			
Lower Limit			
Plus one degree			
Upper Limit			
Assumed Longitude			
LHA			
Convert to "t" angle			
"t" Angle			

STORE IN CALCULATOR		INTERCEPT AZIMUTH	
DR Latitude		Hc A	
Declination		Ho T	
"t" Angle		Intercept (toward away)	

KEY STROKES TI30Xa CALCULATOR			
FIRST EQUATION FOR HEIGHT BY SEXTANT CALCULATED			
Enter memory 1 Lat.	2nd	DMS-DD	STO 1
Enter memory 2 Dec	2nd	DMS-DD	STO 2
Enter memory 3 "t"	2nd	DMS-DD	STO 3
Recall memory 1	RCL	1	SIN
Multiply	X		
Recall memory 2	RCL	2	SIN
Add	+		
Recall memory 1	RCL	1	COS
Multiply	X		
Recall memory 2	RCL	2	COS
Multiply	X		
Recall memory 3	RCL	3	COS
Equal	=		
Invert cosine	2nd	COS	
Store memory 3	STO	3	
Subtract 90°	-	90	
Read Hc			

Wilhelm's School Of Navigation

KEY STROKES TI30Xa CALCULATOR			
SECOND EQUATION FOR AZIMUTH			
Recall memory 2	RCL	2	SIN
Subtract	-		
Recall memory 3	RCL	3	COS
Multiply	X		
Recall memory 1	RCL	1	SIN
Equal	=		
Divide	÷		
Recall memory 3	RCL	3	SIN
Divide	÷		
Recall memory 1	RCL	1	COS
Equal	=		
Invert cosine	2nd	COS	
Read ZN =			

Zone Time for Local Apparent Noon – LAN:

The prediction for LAN depends upon possessing an accurate longitude. In order to conjecture the zone time which depends on navigator's longitude a prior fix update is required. The best method for small ship operation is to use the TI30Xa calculator which allows easy access to Polar Rectangular mathematics.

Illustrative Problem: *On 6 February 1993, DR 26°36.0S, 077°13.0E, zone time 0900 hours, course 258°T, speed 19 knots, navigator observes sun for an LOP. What is zone time for LAN when the assumed position is 28°00.0S, 077°48'.0E?*

COMPUTATION OF TIME ADVANCED:			
Almanac daily white page(right hand side)		Mer-Pass	1214
Zone time last fix (077°13.0 ÷ 15°)		ZT	-1000
Time of advance		TOA	0214

Almanac daily white page Mer-Pass		1214	
Zone time of last fix		-0900	
Time of advance		0314	

TO ADVANCE POSITION			
Explanation		Key Strokes	Lat/Long.
Enter time		3.14	26°36.0S
Convert to decimal		2nd DMS-DD	+00.12.7
Multiply		X	26°48.7S
Vessel's speed		19	+26°36.0S
Equal		=	53°24.7 ÷ 2
Distance traveled		61.143333333	26°42.4 mid-lat
Polar Rectangle		2nd (x-y)	Or 27° mid lat
Vessel's course		258	
Polar Rectangle		2nd (P-R)	
Correction to arrive at DR Latitude		-12.77270821	
Polar Rectangle		2ns (x-y)	
Divide		÷	
Mid-latitude		27	077°13.0E
Cosine of 27 & equal key		COS (=)	-001°07.4
Result – correction for DR longitude		-67.44155736	076°05.6E

Wilhelm's School Of Navigation

SIGHT REDUCTION HO-229 WORKSHEET

Celestial Body		Hs	
Date		Ie	
ZT		He	
ZD (longitude ÷ 15°)		Ha	
GMT		Alt.	
		HP (moon)	
		HO	

GHA		"v / d"	Dec.
GHA whole hour			
GHA m/s			
v/d correction			
GHA			
Dr Longitude			
Less 30'			
Lower Limit			
Plus One degree			
Upper Limit			
aLo			
LHA			
Less 180°			
"t" angle and declination			

Hc		d	Z
HO-229			
Next below z			
Difference			
Minutes of dec. x (10th of z) ÷ 60			
"d" x minutes of dec. ÷ 60			
Hc	A	Sum	
Ho	T	LHA > 180°	
Intercept		Zn	

Wilhelm's School Of Navigation

APPENDIX
SUMMARY OF MATHEMATICAL EQUATIONS

DISTANCE TO HORIZON:

$\sqrt{\text{Height of eye}}$ X 1.14 = Distance to horizon in miles

TIME, SPEED, DISTANCE EQUATIONS:

$$D = \frac{S \times T}{60} \qquad S = \frac{60 \times D}{T} \qquad T = \frac{60 \times D}{S}$$

Solutions for Time, Speed, Distance Problems:

D = distance in miles
S = speed in knots
T = time in minutes

$$D = \text{Speed} \times (\text{Time} \div 60) \qquad S = \frac{D}{(\text{Time} \div 60)} \qquad \text{Time } (T \times 60) = \frac{D}{\text{Speed}}$$

FUEL REQUIREMENT:

$$\frac{\text{Miles First Leg}}{\text{Fuel Consumed}} \quad \text{is to} \quad \frac{\text{Miles Second Leg}}{\text{Expected Consumption}}$$

COMPUTING VESSEL'S PROPELLER SLIPPAGE:

$$\frac{(\text{Propeller RPM} \times 60 \text{ minutes}) \times \text{pitch}}{6076 \text{ feet (1 nautical mile)}} \div \frac{\text{miles traveled}}{\text{time of travel}} = \text{SLIP}$$

REQUIRED RPM WHEN SLIP IS KNOWN:

$$\frac{6076 \times [\text{ vessel's speed} \times (1.0 - \text{negative slip percentage})]}{60 \text{ minutes} \times \text{propeller pitch}} = \text{RPM}$$

Wilhelm's School Of Navigation

MEASUREING DISTANCE:

Departure Latitude = dL(1)
Destination Latitude = dL(2)
Difference in Longitude = dL(3)

Sin dL(1) X dL(2) + Cosin dL(1) X Cosin dL(2) X Cosin dL(3) = [Inv] X 60 = Distance
[cos]

GREAT CIRCLE SAILING:

Departure Latitude = dL(1)
Destination Latitude = dL(2)
Difference in Longitude = dL(3)

Sin dL(1) X dL(2) + Cosin dL(1) X Cosin dL(2) X Cosin dL(3) = [Inv] X 60 = Distance
[cos]

$$\frac{dL(2) - Cosin\ dL(3)\ X\ Sin\ dL(1)}{Sin\ dL(3)\ \&\ Cosin\ dL(1)} = [Inv]\ result\ is\ true\ course\ or\ less\ 360°\ if\ west$$
[cos]

PANE SAILING:

Difference of latitude = Distance X cos Course
Distance East or West of departure = Distance X sin Course

TRANVERSE SAILING:

$$TAN^{-1} = \frac{SOG\ X\ sin\ COG - Speed\ X\ sin\ Course}{SOG\ X\ cos\ COG - Speed\ X\ cos\ Course}$$

$$DRIFT = \frac{SOG\ X\ sin\ COG - Speed\ sin\ Course}{Sin\ Set}$$

PARALLEL SAILING:

$$Difference\ in\ degrees\ of\ longitude = \frac{Distance\ Run}{60\ cos\ Latitude\ (in\ decimal\ degrees)}$$

MERCATOR SAILING:

$$\frac{Difference\ in\ Longitude}{Meridional\ parts} = \frac{Inv}{tan}\ result\ is\ the\ Angle$$

$$\frac{Difference\ in\ Latitude}{Cos\ Angle} = Distance$$

Wilhelm's School Of Navigation

MIDDLE LATITUDE SAILING:

EXAMPLE: *A ship, the American Mariner departs 26°15.0N, 047°15.0W and steams 2h 28m at 21.7k on a true course of 130°. What is latitude and longitude at destination?*

KEY	KEY	DISPLAY	FUNCTION	Mid-Lat.
2.28	2nd DMS-DD	2.466666667	Time in decimal	26°15.0N
X	21.7	21.7	Speed	- 00°34.4S
=	2nd x-y	21.7	Polar rectangle	25°40.6N New Lat.
130	2nd P-R	34.40627812	Lat. difference	+ 26°15.0N
2nd x-y	÷	41.00380556	Polar rectangle	51°55.6 ÷ 2
25.5748	2nd DMS-DD	25.96333333	Mid-Lat. cosin	= 25°57.8N Mid-Lat.
COS	=	45.60668792	Lo. Difference	

047°15.0W
- 000°45.6E
046°29.4W New Lo.

RELATIVE BEARING:

Relative Bearing = RB
Ship's Heading = SH
True Bearing   = TB

RB + SH = TB
TB - SH = RB

LEEWAY & SOG:

D   = drift
RBS = relative bearing of set
S   = vessel's speed

Leeway = $\sin^{-1} \dfrac{D \times \sin RBS}{S}$

SOG = (cosin Leeway X S) + (D X cosin RBS)

CURRENT SAILING-FINDING SET & DRIFT:

$\dfrac{(\text{Speed x sin Course}) + (\text{Drift x sin Set})}{(\text{Speed x sin Course}) + (\text{Drift x sin Set})}$ Inv tan = COG

$\dfrac{(\text{Speed x sin Course}) + (\text{Drift x sin Set})}{\text{Sin COG}}$ = Drift

Wilhelm's School Of Navigation

BEARING & DISTANCE OFF 2nd LOP:

$$\frac{\text{Distance Run x } \sin 1^{st} \text{ relative bearing}}{\sin (1^{st} \text{ relative bearing} - 2^{nd} \text{ relative bearing})} = \text{Distance off at } 2^{nd} \text{ LOP}$$

PASSING MARK PREDETERMINED DISTANCE FROM AFAR:

$$\frac{\text{Distance Off}}{\text{Distance To Go}} = \text{Inv} \quad \text{Result is the}$$
$$\text{Sin} \quad \text{Angle}$$

$$\frac{\text{Distance Off}}{\tan \text{Angle}} = \text{Distance to go (DTG)}$$

$$\frac{\text{Distance to Go}}{\text{Speed}} = \text{Time to Go (TTG)}$$

CORRECTION FOR DIP:

$$\text{Correction for dip} = 0.97 \sqrt{\text{height of eye}}$$

AMPLITUDE:

$$\sin \text{Dec.} - (\cos \text{"}t\text{"} \text{ X } \sin \text{Lat.}) \div \sin \text{"}t\text{"} \div \cos \text{Lat.} = Z \text{ (if "}t\text{" is west -360°)} = Zn$$

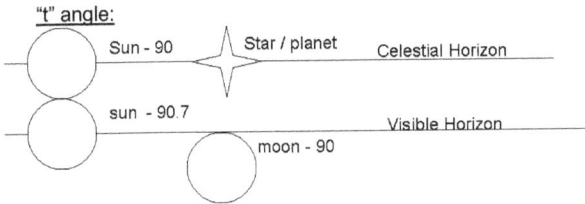

"t" angle:

Sun - 90   Star / planet   Celestial Horizon

sun - 90.7   Visible Horizon

moon - 90

ALTITUDE AZIMUTH:

$$90° - \left\{ \text{Inv} \cos (\sin \text{Lat. X } \sin \text{Dec.} + \cos \text{Lat. X } \cos \text{Dec. X } \cos \text{"t"}) \right\} = HC$$

$$\frac{\sin \text{Dec.} - \cos \text{"t" X } \sin \text{Lat.}}{\sin \text{"t"}} \div \cos \text{Lat.} = ZN \text{ (if west minus 360°)}$$

www.ingramcontent.com/pod-product-compliance
Lightning Source LLC
Chambersburg PA
CBHW060116050426

42448CB00010B/1894